JEAN-PAUL SARTRE

D1251793

A critical figure in twentieth-century literature and philosophy, Jean-Paul Sartre's existentialism changed the course of critical thought, and claimed a new, important role for the intellectual.

Christine Daigle sets Sartre's thought in context, and considers a number of key ideas in detail, charting their impact and continuing influence, including:

- Sartre's theories of consciousness, being and freedom, as outlined in *Being and Nothingness* and other texts
- the ethics of authenticity and absolute responsibility
- concrete relations, sexual relationships and gender difference, focusing on the significance of the alienating look of the Other
- the social and political role of the author
- the legacy of Sartre's theories and their relationship to structuralism and philosophy of mind.

Introducing both literary and philosophical texts by Sartre, this volume makes Sartre's ideas newly accessible to students of literary and cultural studies as well as to students of continental philosophy and French.

Christine Daigle is Associate Professor of Philosophy and Director of the Centre for Women's Studies at Brock University (Ontario, Canada). She is President of the North American Sartre Society (NASS), author of *Le Nihilisme est-il un humanisme: Étude sur Nietzsche et Sartre* (PUL, 2005) and editor of *Existentialist Thinkers and Ethics* (MQUP, 2006).

ROUTLEDGE CRITICAL THINKERS

Series Editor: Robert Eaglestone, Royal Holloway, University of London

Routledge Critical Thinkers is a series of accessible introductions to key figures in contemporary critical thought.

With a unique focus on historical and intellectual contexts, the volumes in this series examine important theorists':

- significance
- motivation
- key ideas and their sources
- impact on other thinkers

Concluding with extensively annotated guides to further reading, *Routledge Critical Thinkers* are the student's passport to today's most exciting critical thought.

Also available in the series:

For further information on this series visit:
www.routledgeliterature.com/books/series

JEAN-PAUL SARTRE

Christine Daigle

LONDON AND NEW YORK

First edition published 2010
by Routledge
2 Park Square, Milton Park, Abingdon, Oxon OX14 4RN

Simultaneously published in the USA and Canada
by Routledge
270 Madison Ave, New York, NY 10016

*Routledge is an imprint of the Taylor & Francis Group, an
informa business*

© 2010 Christine Daigle

Typeset in Series Design Selected by
Taylor & Francis Books
Printed and bound in Great Britain by
TJ International Ltd, Padstow, Cornwall

British Library Cataloguing in Publication Data
A catalogue record for this book is available from the British
Library

Library of Congress Cataloging in Publication Data
Daigle, Christine, 1967–
 Jean-Paul Sartre / by Christine Daigle. – 1st ed.
  p. cm. – (Routledge critical thinkers)
 Includes bibliographical references and index.
 1. Sartre, Jean-Paul, 1905–1980–Criticism and
 interpretation. I. Title.
 PQ2637.A82Z645 2009
848'.91409 –
dc22   2009005888

ISBN10: 0-415-43564-1 (hbk)
ISBN10: 0-415-43565-X (pbk)
ISBN10: 0-203-88273-3 (ebk)

ISBN13: 978-0-415-43564-2 (hbk)
ISBN13: 978-0-415-43565-9 (pbk)
ISBN13: 978-0-203-88273-3 (ebk)

CONTENTS

SERIES EDITOR'S PREFACE

The books in this series offer introductions to major critical thinkers who have influenced literary studies and the humanities. The *Routledge Critical Thinkers* series provides the books you can turn to first when a new name or concept appears in your studies.

Each book will equip you to approach a key thinker's original texts by explaining their key ideas, putting them into context and, perhaps most importantly, showing you why this thinker is considered to be significant. The emphasis is on concise, clearly written guides which do not presuppose a specialist knowledge. Although the focus is on particular figures, the series stresses that no critical thinker ever existed in a vacuum but, instead, emerged from a broader intellectual, cultural and social history. Finally, these books will act as a bridge between you and the thinker's original texts: not replacing them but rather complementing what they wrote. In some cases, volumes consider small clusters of thinkers, working in the same area, developing similar ideas or influencing each other.

These books are necessary for a number of reasons. In his 1997 autobiography, *Not Entitled*, the literary critic Frank Kermode wrote of a time in the 1960s:

> On beautiful summer lawns, young people lay together all night, recovering from their daytime exertions and listening to a troupe of Balinese musicians. Under their blankets or their sleeping bags, they would chat drowsily about the gurus of the time … What they repeated was largely hearsay; hence my lunch-time suggestion, quite impromptu, for a series of short, very cheap books offering authoritative but intelligible introductions to such figures.

There is still a need for 'authoritative and intelligible introductions'. But this series reflects a different world from the 1960s. New thinkers have emerged and the reputations of others have risen and fallen, as new research has developed. New methodologies and challenging ideas have spread through the arts and humanities. The study of literature is no longer – if it ever was – simply the study and evaluation of poems, novels and plays. It is also the study of ideas, issues and difficulties which arise in any literary text and in its interpretation. Other arts and humanities subjects have changed in analogous ways.

With these changes, new problems have emerged. The ideas and issues behind these radical changes in the humanities are often presented without reference to wider contexts or as theories which you can simply 'add on' to the texts you read. Certainly, there's nothing wrong with picking out selected ideas or using what comes to hand – indeed, some thinkers have argued that this is, in fact, all we can do. However, it is sometimes forgotten that each new idea comes from the pattern and development of somebody's thought and it is important to study the range and context of their ideas. Against theories 'floating in space', the *Routledge Critical Thinkers* series places key thinkers and their ideas firmly back in their contexts.

More than this, these books reflect the need to go back to the thinkers' own texts and ideas. Every interpretation of an idea, even the most seemingly innocent one, offers you its own 'spin', implicitly or explicitly. To read only books on a thinker, rather than texts by that thinker, is to deny yourself a chance of making up your own mind. Sometimes what makes a significant figure's work hard to approach is not so much its style or the content as the feeling of not knowing where to start. The purpose of these books is to give you a 'way in' by offering an accessible overview of these thinkers' ideas and works and by guiding your further reading, starting with each thinker's own texts. To use a metaphor from the philosopher Ludwig Wittgenstein (1889–1951), these books are ladders, to be thrown away after you have climbed to the next level. Not only, then, do they equip you to approach new ideas, but also they empower you, by leading you back to the theorist's own texts and encouraging you to develop your own informed opinions.

Finally, these books are necessary because, just as intellectual needs have changed, the education systems around the world – the contexts in which introductory books are usually read – have changed radically, too. What was suitable for the minority higher education systems of the 1960s is not suitable for the larger, wider, more diverse, high technology education systems of the twenty-first century. These changes call not just for new, up-to-date introductions but new methods of presentation. The presentational aspects of *Routledge Critical Thinkers* have been developed with today's students in mind.

Each book in the series has a similar structure. They begin with a section offering an overview of the life and ideas of the featured thinkers and explain why they are important. The central section of each book discusses the thinker's key ideas, their context, evolution, and reception; with the books that deal with more than one thinker, they also explain and explore the influence of each on each. The volumes conclude with a survey of the impact of the thinker or thinkers, outlining how their ideas have been taken up and developed by others. In addition, there is a detailed final section suggesting and describing books for further reading. This is not a 'tacked-on' section but an integral part of each volume. In the first part of this section you will find brief descriptions of the thinker's key works, then, following this, information on the most useful critical works and, in some cases, on relevant websites. This section will guide you in your reading, enabling you to follow your interests and develop your own projects. The books also explain technical terms and use boxes to describe events or ideas in more detail, away from the main emphasis of the discussion. Boxes are also used at times to highlight definitions of terms frequently used or coined by a thinker. In this way, the boxes serve as a kind of glossary, easily identified when flicking through the book.

The thinkers in the series are 'critical' for three reasons. First, they are examined in the light of subjects which involve criticism: principally literary studies or English and cultural studies, but also other disciplines which rely on the criticism of books, ideas, theories and unquestioned assumptions. Second, they are critical because studying their work will provide you with a 'tool kit' for your own informed critical reading and thought, which will make you critical. Third, these thinkers are critical because they are crucially important: they deal with ideas and questions which can overturn conventional understandings of the world, of texts, of everything we take for granted, leaving us with a deeper understanding of what we already knew and with new ideas.

No introduction can tell you everything. However, by offering a way into critical thinking, this series hopes to begin to engage you in an activity which is productive, constructive and potentially life-changing.

ACKNOWLEDGEMENTS

I would like to thank my partner, Eric Gignac, whose understanding is always put to the test when I engage in such long-term projects. Thank you for your continued support. I wish to also thank Dr. Robert Eaglestone, series editor, for his help and encouragement. James Benefield and Polly Dodson at Routledge also deserve my many thanks. Finally, a special thank you goes to Christopher R. Wood, who worked for me as a research assistant on this project. His clear passion for Sartre, knowledge of the material, and enthusiasm for the project were as invaluable as his good diligent work. This book is almost as much his as it is mine.

ABBREVIATIONS

LIST OF SARTRE'S WORKS FREQUENTLY USED:

A-SJ	*Anti-Semite and Jew*
BN	*Being and Nothingness*
Carnets	*Carnets de la drôle de guerre*
Condemned	*The Condemned of Altona*
Devil	*The Devil and the Good Lord*
Écrits	*Les Écrits de Jean-Paul Sartre*
EH	*Existentialism is a Humanism*
Flies	*The Flies*
Iron	*Iron in the Soul*
Itinerary	*"Itinerary of a Thought"*
N	*Nausea*
No Exit	*No Exit*
Notebooks	*Notebooks for an Ethics*
Présentation	*"Présentation des Temps modernes"*
SM	*Search for a Method*
TE	*Transcendence of the Ego*
Théâtre	*Un Théâtre de situations*
WD	*War Diaries*
WL	*What is Literature?*
Words	*Words*

WHY SARTRE?

"A whole man, made of all men, worth all of them,
and any one of them worth him." (*Words*)

These are Sartre's final words to his autobiography, but Sartre was certainly more than just anybody. A key figure of twentieth-century philosophy and literature, this icon of existentialist philosophy presented his contemporaries and the generations that followed with complex writings, rich in new ideas. These were meant to replace the alienating world-view inherited from past centuries of religious discourse and rationalistic philosophizing. Claiming that the human being is fundamentally free and makes himself according to his projects, Sartre proposed a view that centered around the notion of absolute freedom and choice. Empowering to the individual, this view was also highly demanding and required not only private but also public engagement. Sartre himself was a politically committed individual: existentialism is no ivory-tower philosophy; it is a philosophy for actual individuals in the real world.

Sartre's ideas truly changed the face of philosophy and literature, and attributed a new and important role to the intellectual. His thought has thus been influential in many ways; it serves as a hinge to the development of philosophy in the twentieth century. One may say that his writings represent the peak of the theorization of existentialism as a philosophical movement—as the main representative of existentialism, Sartre is also the last major one. His philosophy of consciousness, which is no longer a philosophy of the rational subject, opens the door to philosophical and literary movements like deconstructionism, structuralism, and poststructuralism that followed him. It is safe to say that, without Sartre's key work, *Being and Nothingness*, these movements would not exist as we know them.

SARTRE IN CONTEXT

Jean-Paul Sartre was born on June 21, 1905, in Paris. His father, Jean-Baptiste, died when he was only 15 months old. His widowed young mother, Anne-Marie, returned to the home of her parents, Charles and Louise Schweitzer (related to famous missionary and humanitarian Albert Schweitzer). Sartre's grandfather, Charles (Karl in Sartre's autobiography, *Words*) was a teacher of German and well-known pedagogue. "Poulou," Sartre's childhood nickname in the Schweitzer household, was thus raised in a bourgeois intellectual environment. He found the perfect place to flourish in this household that favored intellectual activities and pursuits. Admired by all in the household, schooled in his early years by his grandfather and known to spend hours surrounded by books in his study, the young Sartre immersed himself in the world of the great classics of literature at a very early age.

SARTRE'S ATTRACTION TO LITERATURE

In his early years, living in the grandfather's household and surrounded by books, Sartre could cater to his longing for literature. He was also drawn to comic books, and was a big fan of the *Nick Carter* detective stories. He would purchase issues of his favorite series when going out with his mother to the park and to the movies. He tried to hide these "guilty pleasures" from his grandfather who, as the patriarch, was the absolute authority. The grandfather did not approve of such cheap entertainment.

Sartre was drawn to literature at a very early age; his literary talent was just waiting to bud. His environment certainly contributed to this budding. In his autobiography, he recounts that he naturally grew out of reading into a writer and undertook to write his own pieces. At first, he copied down some stories and then ventured to compose short stories and even plays for puppet shows. His mother was very supportive of the little writer neatly copying his creations and doing public readings of them.

That Sartre's autobiography is titled *Les Mots* (Words) is telling of how he saw himself literally as possessed by words and literature. He said: "I began my life as I shall no doubt end it: among books" (Words 30).

After some difficult years in La Rochelle as a teenager, and after his mother had remarried, Sartre returned to Paris in 1920 as a boarder at the Lycée Henri IV. There, he befriended Paul Nizan, with whom an intense relationship would unfold over seven years. They were so close that schoolmates would refer to them as "Nitre et Sarzan." In 1924, he entered the École Normale Supérieure.

This period was much happier for Sartre as he was shaping up intellectually and personally, and developing important friendships such as the one with Nizan but also with Raymond Aron (1905–83), who was to become an important French intellectual, and Simone de Beauvoir (1908–86) in 1929.

ÉCOLE NORMALE SUPÉRIEURE

Located on rue d'Ulm in Paris, the ENS was founded in 1794. It was, and still is, a very prestigious institution to attend in order to earn a university degree and one that can be attended only once one has succeeded a difficult entry competition. Many important and famous figures attended this school: chemist and biologist Louis Pasteur (1822–95), philosopher Henri Bergson (1859–1941), sociologist Émile Durkheim (1858–1917), Raymond Aron, philosopher Maurice Merleau-Ponty (1908–61), politically committed writer Aimé Césaire (1913–2008), philosopher Simone Weil (1909–43), philosopher Michel Foucault (1926–84), sociologist Pierre Bourdieu (1930–2002), philosopher Jacques Derrida (1930–2004), and, of course, Jean-Paul Sartre.

Initially, there were two parts to the ENS, one for men on the rue d'Ulm, and one for women. The two institutions were fused only recently in 1985.

Beauvoir met Sartre when they were both preparing for the aggregation (the comprehensive examination that would allow them to teach in the French schooling system) in 1929. She was to become his life partner. They never married or even lived together, and had what they called an "open relationship." Sartre had suggested to her that their love was a necessary one, but that they could still enjoy "contingent loves," which they did. While they were free to engage in other relationships, they never ever considered the thought of being separated from one another. They would spend time with each other each day, if possible; if not, they would write lengthy letters to each other. Beauvoir said of Sartre that he was the double she had been seeking for years. Many of Sartre's works are dedicated "au Castor" (for the Beaver). This was Beauvoir's nickname, attributed to her by her friend René Maheu, who thought that the English name, close to her French one, was representative of her constructive character. The encounter with "the Beaver," needless to say, impacted Sartre's life to its end.

Sartre considered Beauvoir not only his equal intellectually but oftentimes referred to her as his intellectual superior. He often remarked that she was more intelligent than he and whenever he wrote a piece—literary or philosophical—it was to her that he turned for a critical reading and advice. She did the same with her own writings. They were each other's first reader, and provided fierce critique. That they were so close intellectually is shown by the results of their aggregation. Sartre had failed at his first attempt in 1928, having been guilty of too much originality. When he did it again, in 1929, he ranked first and Beauvoir second, but the jury hesitated and deliberated at length: they thought that she was the more rigorous philosopher of the two.

After receiving his aggregation, Sartre took up a position as a lycée professor in a small town. He was later drafted in World War II as a simple soldier and served in a meteorological unit. Without ever having seen combat, he was made a prisoner of war (POW) in 1940. He was released in 1941 and went back to Paris. He came back convinced that he must get involved in the Résistance.

THE RÉSISTANCE

Early under the German occupation of France, in 1940 and 1941, many underground organizations were formed to resist it. Some French people who had fled to London broadcasted radio shows on the BBC to communicate information to their countrymen (beginning their broadcasts with "Here is London! French people talk to the French"). These groups were engaged in a number of activities: some would carry out violent attacks in Paris, bombing the train tracks to disrupt German transport, while others concentrated on securing information for the Allies. In 1944, they were instrumental in securing support for the troops that were to invade Normandy and they helped prepare and launch the insurrection of Paris in 1944.

The war had transformed a rather apolitical, anarchist pacifist Sartre into one who believed in the necessity of commitment. After some rather unsuccessful attempts at being involved directly in the Résistance (see Chapter 7), he decided to focus on his writing. From then on, he led the life of an intellectual in Paris: writing in cafés and engaging in discussions with other intellectuals and artists of his days. Sartre could be found at the Café de Flore or Les Deux Magots on the Boulevard St-Germain, often surrounded by an intellectual and artistic fauna composed of such people as artists Pablo Picasso (1881–1973), Boris Vian (1920–59), Alberto Giacometti (1901–66), Salvador Dalí (1904–89), and philosophers and writers Simone de Beauvoir, Maurice Merleau-Ponty, and Albert Camus (1913–60).

In 1945, existentialism was the buzzword. As its main representative, Sartre was propelled to the centre of public attention. He gave conferences, published articles, and was interviewed. Sartre and Beauvoir were the two main figures of this incredibly popular—but often misunderstood—movement. Sartre's public conference at Le Club Maintenant (the "Now Club"), on October 29, 1945, consecrated his and existentialism's notoriety.

BORIS VIAN'S ABSURD ACCOUNT OF "EXISTENTIALISM IS A HUMANISM"

In his novel *Foam of the Daze* (1947), Boris Vian, a friend of Sartre, gives a fictional absurd humorous account of the famous conference pronounced at Le Club Maintenant. The main character of the novel, Chick, is the greatest fan of Jean-Sol Partre and collector of any item related to

Partre, including meal leftovers and old, worn-out suits. He arranges to replace a friend to work at the theater where Partre is going to give his important conference. The impatient crowd uses all kinds of stratagems to get inside the room, from fake invitations to crawling through the sewer system, arriving in hearses (and promptly nailed by steel spikes poked by policemen), to parachuting in. As the crowd is growing impatient for the conference to begin, Partre arrives:

> But, Jean-Sol was approaching. Elephant trumpet sounds were heard coming from the street and Chick leaned out the window of his box seat. In the distance, the silhouette of Jean-Sol emerged from the armored howdah under which the back of the elephant, rough and wrinkled, took on a strange air in the glow of a red beacon. At each corner of the howdah was a sniper armed with a hatchet and ready to act. With great strides, the elephant made its way through the crowd and the dull stamping sound of the four pillars trudging through the crushed bodies was getting inexorably closer. In front of the door, the elephant kneeled down and the snipers descended. With a graceful bound, Partre leapt out into the middle of them, and, clearing a path by blows of their hatchets, they progressed toward the rostrum.
>
> (*Foam of the Daze* 90–1)

This rather grandiose and dramatic entrance is followed by the conference. The crowd is frantic. "Numerous were the cases of fainting brought on by the intra-uterine exaltation that took hold more particularly of the feminine element of the audience, [...]" (ibid. 91). All that unfolds is more and more absurd and chaotic, with Partre showing samples of vomit (a direct reference to Sartre's novel *Nausea*) and the ceiling falling down due to the weight of "audacious admirers" who had crawled into it to listen. Partre laughs, swallows dust, chokes, "The pandemonium in the room was at the breaking point (95)." Chick invites Partre to leave through the back door.

While Vian's account is absurd and clearly exaggerates the event, it nonetheless conveys the utter enthusiasm with which Sartre's philosophy and literature was received at the close of World War II and at this specific popular event.

By that time, Sartre was a well-known novelist, playwright and philosopher and he was the director of the new journal, *Les Temps modernes*. He was constantly in the public eye, publishing many articles and continuing to write novels, plays and philosophical essays. He was increasingly involved in political discussions and fierce critique. He had socialist leanings but, although he was sometimes close to the Communist party, he was never a member, preferring to maintain his independence and to be a "road companion." Because of his notoriety, Sartre was often solicited to support social causes and movements. He often did so, and participated directly in marches and protests. There are numerous pictures of Sartre and Beauvoir taking active part in public manifestations. One of the most famous probably is that of Sartre standing on a barrel at the Renaud plant in Billancourt in 1970, speaking to the workers and thus actualizing his position as the committed intellectual who speaks directly to and with the people.

Sartre was a public figure in France but also abroad. He travelled around the world and met with important leaders. He was interested and attracted by communism and visited the USSR, as well as the Eastern bloc and China. He met with revolutionaries and new leaders Fidel Castro and Che Guevara in Cuba, Soviet leader Nikita Krushchev, Yugoslav leader Marshal Tito, and China's president Mao Zedong. He was involved in all political discussions and all struggles. He was very active, for example, in supporting the former French colony of Algeria in its struggle to free itself from France. His support triggered much negative reaction in France, and many campaigned against Sartre. However, when asked about Sartre's participation and whether he should be jailed, General Charles de Gaulle, then President of France, objected, "One does not jail Voltaire!" Sartre's position with regards to the Algerian war triggered passionate reactions, so much so that his apartment was bombed in 1961. Sartre's writings and political commitments left no one indifferent, up until the end of his life. He protested against the war in Vietnam, supported the student uprising in May 1968, and contributed to the launching of the press agency *Libération* and its newspaper in the early 1970s. All the while, literature called on him. He continued his work on Gustave Flaubert but had to interrupt it when he lost his sight in 1973 (the three volumes of *The Family Idiot* were published in 1971 and 1972, but Sartre was not able to write his planned fourth volume). Although he could no longer write, Sartre could still make use of his notoriety to intervene publicly. This he did until the end of his life, when, blind and ill, he joined with Raymond Aron in June 1979 to request more support from the French President for Vietnam's boat people. On April 15, 1980, he died at the age of 74. On the day of his funeral, an immense crowd (estimated at 50,000) followed his coffin through the streets of Paris to the Montparnasse cemetery, demonstrating Sartre's importance and stature in French intellectual and cultural life.

SARTRE AS "TOTAL INTELLECTUAL"

Sartre is not only a philosopher and a writer; he is much more. A quick overview of his writings will give us a sense of the scope of his intellectual activity. In 1936, his first philosophical essays were published: *Imagination* and *Transcendence of the Ego*. In the latter essay, Sartre was positioning himself vis-à-vis German philosopher and phenomenologist Edmund Husserl (1859–1938), and beginning to elaborate his own philosophy of consciousness. In 1938, the novel *Nausea* was published by Gallimard. This was the beginning of a lifelong collaboration with Gallimard, which would publish most of Sartre's works. He published a collection of short stories, *The Wall*, as well as his *Sketch for a Theory of Emotions* in 1939, and began to work on the novel *The Roads to Freedom*. He was drafted in September 1939, but continued to work on his novel and began drafts of what was to become *Being and Nothingness*. The latter would be published in 1943 and the first two volumes of *The Roads to Freedom* were published in 1945.

Sartre had written his first play while in the POW camp in 1940 and, when it was staged for Christmas, he discovered theater's power of communication. Following the war, he wrote many plays. *The Flies* was staged in 1943, *No Exit* in 1944, *Morts sans sépultures* (translated as *The Victors* and *Men Without Shadows*) in 1946, *The Respectful Prostitute* in 1946, *Dirty Hands* in 1948, *The Devil and the Good Lord* in 1951, *Nekrassov* in 1955, and *The Condemned of Altona* in 1959. He also adapted two plays: one by Alexandre Dumas, *Kean*, staged in 1953, and the other by Euripides, *The Trojans*, staged in 1965. His theater was the occasion for him to revisit his philosophical ideas and present them to the public in a different form. While not a didactic theater, Sartre's theater is one that makes the audience think about the human condition and reflect about important ethical problems.

The 1940s was the decade when Sartre began writing for theater and cinema. His attraction to cinema was not new; as a young boy he was already fascinated by movies. As a young professor in Le Havre, he had given talks about movies and cinema. In 1943, he was hired by the production company Pathé to write scenarios, some of which found their way to the screen. In 1958, he agreed to collaborate with American filmmaker John Huston (1906–87) to write a scenario on the life of Austrian psychoanalyst Sigmund Freud (1856–1939). Sartre worked on two versions of the script, both too long for Huston to use. The movie was made, but only after many revisions and edits to Sartre's script, after which he asked that his name be taken out of the generic. The original scenario was published later.

In the 1940s, Sartre also began to write articles for newspapers and journals about current topics and affairs. He wrote for *Les Temps modernes*, but also, and before *Les Temps modernes* was launched, for *Combat* (edited by Albert Camus), *Le Figaro*, and later for other papers and journals. A series of 10 collections of Sartre's essays titled *Situations* gives a small sample of this wide range of essays (they were published between 1947 and 1976). Sartre reflected on all aspects of the world and shared his views in his writings. Philosophical treatises and literary pieces needed to be complemented by these more punctual and circumstantial interventions.

All the while, Sartre continued his philosophical and literary enterprise. Following the publication of *Being and Nothingness* in 1943, he published the essay *Anti-Semite and Jew* in 1946, and the text of the public conference *Existentialism is a Humanism* in 1946. In 1947 and 1948, he worked on an ethics treatise, a project that he later abandoned. In 1949, the third volume of *The Roads to Freedom* was published. He wrote the preface to the works of French dramatist Jean Genet (1910–86). What was supposed to be a simple preface ended up being a volume of its own and was published in 1952. The essay represented an evolution in Sartre's philosophical thought. The 1950s saw Sartre focus his reflection on historical, ethical, and political issues. He was revising some of his earlier views and also revisited his formative years by working on his autobiography, *Words*, which would be published in 1963. In 1957, he published *Questions of Method*, a text that encompassed the essay "Marxism and Existentialism," which he had published in a Polish journal earlier in the year. When Sartre's second major philosophical text was published in 1960, *The Critique of Dialectical Reason*, he used *Questions of Method* as a preface.

Following the publication of the *Critique of Dialectical Reason* and *Words*, the only major work that Sartre undertook, alongside all his numerous writing activities, was the study on the nineteenth-century French novelist Gustave Flaubert (1821–80). Entitled *The Family Idiot*, it was published in three volumes in 1971–2. To this already impressive list of writings, one must also add material that was either published posthumously (including the bulk of letters that Sartre wrote to Beauvoir and others, published posthumously by Beauvoir herself; his *War Diaries*; his study on Mallarmé, the *Notebooks for an Ethics*) as well as some material that has been lost (for example, a study on Nietzsche that Sartre would have written as part of his ethics project as well as other notebooks from the war that were lost).

The picture that emerges from this necessarily incomplete review of Sartre's works is that of an intellectual who grasped everything within his reach. Talented and with a voracious mind, he devoted himself to his writing. He was a total intellectual, in that his activity was not confined to one realm or style. He was fully committed and believed that, as a writer, he had an important social role to play (we will discuss this in detail in Chapter 7).

INTELLECTUAL CONTEXT

Sartre's thought and writings emerged within a particular intellectual context. Specifically, his philosophy inscribed itself in the movement of existential thought that had emerged in the nineteenth century with the writings of Danish philosopher Søren Kierkegaard (1813–55) and German philosopher Friedrich Nietzsche (1844–1900). These thinkers' new approach and focus on the human individual were influential on Sartre. But it is important to keep in mind that Sartre was trained in traditional philosophy. Descartes' rationalist philosophy remained a crucial influence on him even if only in his effort to revise and reject Cartesianism (something we will discuss in further chapters). Sartre had studied the works of Dutch philosopher Baruch Spinoza (1632–77), rationalist German philosophers Immanuel Kant (1724–1804) and Friedrich Hegel (1770–1831), as well as those of Nietzsche. All found their way into his writings, often as a springboard for his own ideas. They acted as allies or as counterpoises to his views.

TRADITIONAL RATIONALIST PHILOSOPHY

The philosophical tradition in which Sartre was trained is that of rationalism. With its roots in Plato's philosophy, as famously exposed in *The Republic*, rationalism posits that the human being is first and foremost a "rational animal," and greatly emphasizes this aspect of the individual. In one of his dialogues, for example, it is said that the philosopher's rational soul despises the body and tries to flee it. René Descartes (1596–1650), another famous rationalist, also introduced a sharp distinction between body and mind, focusing on the mind as the one thing that characterizes human beings. The body is essentially treated as an instrument for them. Kant and Hegel, other major figures of rationalism, also focused their attention on the human being qua mind.

Rationalism's whole emphasis on the subject as rational is too dismissive of the passions and of the body for existentialist thinkers, however. They reject this with their view of the individual. As we will see, this is also the case with Sartre, who will revisit and reformulate the rationalist motto proposed by Descartes: "I think, therefore I am" (see Chapter 1).

German philosophy beyond Hegel was also instrumental in the development of Sartre as an existential phenomenologist. As we will come to see in Chapter 2, it was on the basis of his study of Edmund Husserl's works that Sartre first elaborated his views on consciousness. His reading of German phenomenologist Martin Heidegger (1889–1976) would also play a very important role, especially in the elaboration of *Being and Nothingness*. In his *magnum opus*, Hegel, Husserl, and Heidegger are frequent interlocutors. Sartre was at pains to show their views and how his own differed from theirs and, in many ways, solved certain problems they had failed to address correctly. When Sartre later turned to political thinking, the influence of political thinker Karl Marx (1818–83) was tremendous. I have said already that Sartre was tempted by socialism. In Marx's writings, he found many elements to articulate his own views of the human being in the social world. We will discuss this in detail in Chapter 8.

Sartre's thinking was born out of this background. But his interaction with contemporaries played an equally important role in shaping his ideas. Most importantly, his discussions and exchange of ideas with Simone de Beauvoir played a key role. Beauvoir too was an existentialist.

Her writings on ethics, *Pyrrhus and Cinéas* (1944) and *The Ethics of Ambiguity* (1947), led Sartre to rethink some of his views on freedom (which we will discuss in Chapter 3). Her theorizing of alterity and oppression (in her novel *She Came to Stay* [1943] but, most notably, in her essay *The Second Sex* [1949]) was akin to some of Sartre's own developments but also, at certain points, well ahead of him. It can be argued that the interchange between the two brought them to the view that one must will one's freedom and, by extension, the freedom of others (which we will discuss in Chapters 3, 5, and 6).

The phenomenologist Maurice Merleau-Ponty, for his part, did not think that Sartre's commitment to Marxism and communism was sufficient. They met at the ENS, but it was really after Sartre was released from the POW camp that they became close, forming the ephemeral resistance group "Socialisme et Liberté" (Socialism and Freedom). In 1945, an offspring of that earlier association was the journal *Les Temps modernes*. Merleau-Ponty was a member of the first editorial team. The multiplicity of political views that the journal presented pleased Merleau-Ponty. He was closer to the Communist party than Sartre was at the time. At the beginning of the 1950s, Merleau-Ponty wrote an article denouncing the Soviet work camps. Sartre, for his part, was drawn closer to the Communist party by the outbreak of the Korean war. This division with regards to their positioning vis-à-vis the Communist party and the Soviet Union triggered the break between them. They were philosophically close, yet different, each elaborating a phenomenological view that had its roots in Husserl's philosophy, but it was politics that ended up dividing them.

Albert Camus was also an important interlocutor for Sartre. They encountered each other in the realm of literature. Camus had reviewed Sartre's novel *Nausea* and the collection of short stories *The Wall* for an Algerian newspaper. Sartre was impressed by Camus' talent as it was expressed in *The Stranger* (1942). After they had met and become friends, Camus asked Sartre to collaborate on the newspaper he was editing, *Combat*. Camus' plays are what Sartre coins "théâtre de situations" (situational theater), much like his own. They also shared some philosophical ideas. *The Myth of Sisyphus* (also published in 1942) was an essay in which Camus analyzed the notion of the absurd, a notion akin to that of contingency that Sartre had presented in his novel *Nausea*. Politically, they stood close enough to publish articles alongside one another on issues pertaining to democracy in

1948 for a special issue of the journal *Franchise* (literally: truthfulness). However, there were already certain disagreements. When Camus published his essay *The Rebel* in 1951, the positions he adopted therein were clearly different than those of Sartre: Camus was the proponent of a moral revolution rather than an actual one, something that Sartre favored more and more as he drew closer to communism. The review of Camus' essay, written by Francis Jeanson and published in *Les Temps modernes*, marked the occasion of the split between Sartre and Camus. This public parting of ways, through Camus' letter to Sartre as the director of the journal, and Sartre's response to Camus published in the same journal, was a major event on the French intellectual scene. Indeed, Sartre and Camus were regarded as the main figures of existential literature and theater.

No thinker can ever flourish and develop in a vacuum; Sartre was no exception. It was his encounter with these philosophies as well as his reading of key literary figures, such as French novelists Stendhal (1783–1842), Flaubert, Marcel Proust (1871–1922), and French poet Charles Baudelaire (1821–67), and many others that shaped his own thinking.

THIS BOOK

In this book, I will focus on what I consider to be Sartre's major contribution to philosophy and literature: his existentialism and philosophy of freedom. In *Existentialism is a Humanism*, Sartre explained that existentialism takes human subjectivity as its starting point. This is what we shall do by launching our investigation of key ideas by an examination of the theory of consciousness that lies at the ground of Sartre's philosophy. Chapter 1 will explain this theory and show how Sartre's views were radically different from those of his predecessors. Chapter 2 will examine Sartre's ontology, or theory of being, as presented in his *magnum opus*, *Being and Nothingness*. This will also be the occasion for us to investigate Sartre's embrace of atheism and its implications for his philosophy of freedom. This will lead us naturally to examine the notion of freedom as presented by Sartre in this treatise and also in his novels and plays: that freedom entails responsibility is an essential existentialist tenet and one that Sartre substantiated in his works. This will be the subject of Chapter 3. Chapter 4 will take a turn toward the ethical implications of Sartre's fundamental positions by examining the notion of authenticity and its correlate, bad faith. This discussion will unfold into an analysis of interpersonal relations as conceived by Sartre, the subject of Chapter 5, which leads us on to whether indeed, "Hell is other people!," as is famously claimed in the play *No Exit*. Chapter 6 will summarize the notions tackled thus far, and discuss the human condition and the ethics of freedom that emerge in Sartre's existentialist writings. In Chapter 7, we will see how Sartre's views on freedom unfolded into a view of literature as committed, i.e., as playing a political role. As a writer, Sartre thought he bore a certain social and political responsibility. We will look into his explanations for that. Chapter 8 will consider how Sartre's theoretical positions entail his own concrete political engagement. Finally, the concluding chapter, "After Sartre," will examine the impact Sartre's thought has had on his contemporaries, the importance of his thought for who followed him, as well as its relevance for thinking our world today.

KEY IDEAS

1

CONSCIOUSNESS

Sartre's existentialism rests upon a theoretical view of consciousness that is crucial to understand. "Human subjectivity is our starting point," says Sartre, and this subjectivity is to be conceived in a way that differs from classical rationalist views such as Descartes'. Where Descartes uncovered his first truth via the experience of the *cogito*, "I think, therefore I am," Sartre digs further down in the depths of subjectivity and uncovers a multi-layered consciousness for which the *cogito* is just one facet. An important factor that led Sartre on this path was his discovery of the German phenomenological movement.

COGITO ERGO SUM

Sartre has acknowledged the influence of Descartes on his own approach to philosophy. In his *Discourse on Method* and *Meditations on First Philosophy*, Descartes sought a way to obtain certain absolute truths in order to provide himself with an unshakable foundation for future knowledge. Dismissing any idea that appeared unclear or questionable, he arrived at the one fundamental truth that he could not possibly reject or doubt: "*cogito, ergo sum*" (or "I think, therefore I am"). This first truth—that he exists as a thinking substance—served as a basis to admit other truths and build his knowledge. This is deemed to be a *rationalist* view insofar as the subject that exists is seen as a thinking substance, i.e. a being that has reason, and that all knowledge obtained by this subject derives from reason alone—not from the external world. Sartre rejects this view as being reductive, and proposes a more comprehensive view of subjectivity as being wholly intertwined with the concrete world.

In this chapter, we will examine how Sartre adopted phenomenology, and how he devised his views about consciousness. We will examine in detail how Sartre explains the nature of consciousness and self-consciousness, and see how his views in this regard entail a rejection of the unconscious. We will also consider how one of Sartre's literary characters, Antoine Roquentin, suffers from nausea, and what it means for him as an existing individual.

PHENOMENOLOGY

Returning from a study year at the Institut Français de Berlin, Raymond Aron explained to Sartre how he could obtain funds to study there. He also suggested to Sartre that he study the work of German phenomenologists. Dissatisfied with traditional philosophical systems and their overly rationalistic and idealistic stances, Sartre was enthusiastic to discover that there existed a type of philosophy that allowed him to talk about concrete things—about the things themselves. This is what attracted him to the philosophy of Edmund Husserl. At the end of his year's stay in Berlin, and after investing much effort in studying phenomenology, Sartre wrote the essay *The Transcendence of the Ego*, in which he explores the inner workings of consciousness for the first time.

EDMUND HUSSERL (1859–1938)

Often considered as the father of phenomenology, Husserl had started his academic career in the field of mathematics. His *Habilitationsschrift* (akin to a postdoctoral thesis) was on a topic in arithmetic. His first comprehensive development of phenomenology was published in 1913 under the title *Ideen I* and underwent numerous transformations throughout his academic career. Husserl's philosophy is quite complex and influenced many twentieth-century thinkers. Following him, different trends of

Husserl's aim was to investigate what remains when one takes the external world away from consciousness and the activity of reflecting, the *cogitare*. He was interested in the sphere of "absolute consciousness," and wanted to uncover what meaning this world has when we see it as it actually exists. For Husserl, phenomenology is the science of essential being. By "bracketing off" certain things from consciousness, he hoped to arrive at the essence of things. If consciousness is always conscious of something, then when one takes away the world, one is left with a pure conscious life that is antecedent to the natural being of the world. This is what Husserl called "bracketing," or *Epoché*. It is the method by which one suspends one's judgments about the natural world in order to access things as they really are. When one is conscious of something, i.e. of the world, one finds intentionality. Using bracketing, Husserl was trying to uncover the nature of pure consciousness, i.e. pure intentionality.

Intentionality is the fundamental property of consciousness. It is consciousness that is conscious of something, consciousness as a *cogito*. Husserl saw that this intentionality is a movement by which consciousness moves out of itself, however. It throws itself out into the world by being conscious of some*thing*. Interestingly, that is what set Husserl apart from Descartes, who was also much concerned with the *cogito*. Descartes thought that the world is not necessary for the *cogito* to go on thinking. Husserl, on the contrary, considered that a world is needed to have a *cogito*, because consciousness, by its very nature, is that flow of intentionality. Both Descartes and Husserl, however, conceived of the ego as the ground that unifies consciousness. Consciousness has experiences, is conscious *of*, and thereby fills itself, existing as this stream of experiences. Descartes and Husserl agree that the ego is an entity that ties these experiences together, that provides a unity of experience. Sartre dismisses this idea and denies that this role belongs to the ego. Consciousness *is* that stream and nothing unifies it but itself; the ego is only a worldly by-product of conscious activity. He says:

> The World has not created the me; the me has not created the World. These are two objects for absolute, impersonal consciousness, and it is by virtue of this consciousness that they are connected. This absolute consciousness,

when it is purified of the I, no longer has anything of the subject. It is no longer a collection of representations. It is quite simply a first condition and an absolute source of existence.

(TE 105–6).

INTENTIONALITY

It was the German philosopher Franz Brentano (1838–1917) who first proposed the idea of intentionality. Husserl used it but diverged from its original Brentanian sense. Sartre's use of intentionality is closer to the original meaning given to it by Brentano as a structure of consciousness: consciousness exists only as conscious (of) something. Thus, consciousness depends on an external world for its existence. Husserl, however, thought that there is such a thing as a pure absolute consciousness—an idea that Sartre criticized him for. Sartre conceives of all modes of consciousness as intentional: knowledge, imagination, emotion, etc. are all intentional structures of consciousness in that they all aim consciousness toward an object external to it. Consciousness is thus, by its very structure, a transcendence (see Chapter 2).

"THERE IS CONSCIOUSNESS"

In the *Transcendence of the Ego*, Sartre explains how he revises the traditional rationalistic conception of the human being. He also critically reappropriates Husserl. As Hazel Barnes puts it, this revision is extremely important because his rejection of Descartes and his fundamental claim about the pre-reflective *cogito* form the "original point of departure" for his thought. (See her discussion of the essay *The Transcendence of the Ego* in Barnes, Hazel, "Translator's Introduction," *Being and Nothingness*, x–xv.) In this essay, Sartre engages in a process of introspection wherein he describes the three steps to one's self-discovery: there is 1. consciousness (as consciousness *of* something); 2. the non-consciousness (the world as being what consciousness is conscious *of*); and 3. the body, the self (what is not the world).

Although the first thing we encounter in this introspective inquiry is consciousness itself, Sartre dissociates himself from traditional idealism. Indeed, he is not claiming that reality has its foundation in consciousness, as idealism holds; rather, he says that the first thing we encounter is consciousness, but it is not consciousness that creates and sustains the world. Consciousness depends on the necessary pre-existence of the world in order to exist. Because it exists as conscious *of* something, this something must already be there for consciousness to be conscious of it. Sartre explains that "consciousness is born supported by a being which is not itself" (BN 23). Again, the discovery that consciousness undergoes unfolds in the following manner: consciousness is conscious of something; this something is the world; the world in turn informs consciousness that it is not the world. This is an epistemological process, i.e. it speaks of the order of acquisition of knowledge, and its results are not of an ontological nature, since it does not say anything about the order of appearances of things as things that exist. It does not say that there is first consciousness, then the world. The world is primary: it is there to be grasped by consciousness. Consciousness does not create the world *ex nihilo*, i.e. from nothing, but rather creates what is already there by interpreting it.

Sartre proposes that consciousness is always also self-consciousness. When I am conscious, my consciousness is conscious of itself as being conscious *of* something. "Thus by nature all consciousness is self-consciousness" (Barnes xiv). This pre-reflective consciousness is without an ego. It is not personal, it is simply consciousness that is conscious *of*. It is consciousness as an act: the act of being conscious, of grasping the world as opposed to consciousness as an object, like a mind or concrete brain. Sartre will therefore want to transform the classical Cartesian formula, "I think, therefore I am," and change it to "There is consciousness, therefore I am." The first "truth" that one uncovers via introspection is the fact of consciousness which is not yet an "I." Again, it is important to stress how much this position differs from that of Descartes or Husserl.

TOPOLOGY OF CONSCIOUSNESS

Sartre presents us with a complex view of consciousness as he explains that there are three levels of consciousness in the human being. The first level is that of *pre-reflective consciousness*, which is consciousness *of* something (consciousness as act). It is the rawest level of consciousness. The second level is that of *reflective consciousness*, and the third is that of *self-reflective consciousness*, where consciousness becomes its own object. Sartre illustrates the differences between them with two examples. Let us examine the example of reading. There he explains that when you are engaged in the act of reading, you are also conscious of the room you are in, the temperature of the room, the chair on which you sit, etc., all on a pre-reflective level. But you are also actively engaged in the reading, which is a reflective activity that requires the second level of consciousness. As a reflective conscious-ness, you are using reflection to be conscious of something in a different way. You read this book: you decipher the signs on the page, you make sense of them, you think about them. These are all reflective ways to be conscious. At the same time, you can also think of yourself as reading, which is self-reflective consciousness. As you are reflectively conscious of reading, i.e. actively thinking about your reading, you are conscious of yourself as a reading-self. You can reflect upon yourself as engaged reflectively in the activity of reading. This is the topology of con-sciousness that Sartre puts forth. According to him, this is how con-sciousness functions. Although he presents these levels of consciousness in a sequence, they should not be thought to "happen" one after the other. These are contemporaneous moments of consciousness.

1. Pre-reflective:

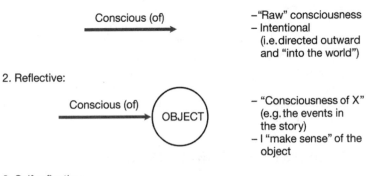

Conscious (of)

– "Raw" consciousness
– Intentional
   (i.e. directed outward
   and "into the world")

2. Reflective:

Conscious (of) OBJECT

– "Consciousness of X"
   (e.g. the events in
   the story)
– I "make sense" of the
   object

3. Self-reflective:

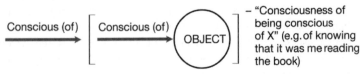

Conscious (of) Conscious (of) OBJECT

– "Consciousness of
   being conscious
   of X" (e.g. of knowing
   that it was me reading
   the book)

Figure 1

Sartre concludes this analysis with a statement that comes pretty close to Merleau-Ponty's view of the body-subject. He explains that, when I am engaged in any action, as in the act of reading, "I am then plunged into the world of objects; it is they which constitute the unity of my consciousnesses […] but *me*, I have disappeared; I have annihilated myself. There is no place for *me* on this level." (TE 49). Objects in the world constitute consciousness. There is a unity of consciousness, and the unifying thread is intentionality, i.e. consciousness as conscious *of* something. This all happens without an ego being in charge; there is no rational, personal process at work in this. There is consciousness as conscious of something in the three different modes indicated above, pre-reflective, reflective, and self-reflective.

MERLEAU-PONTY'S BODY-SUBJECT

Like Sartre, Merleau-Ponty significantly revises the Cartesian (and the Husserlian) *cogito*. He says: "our body is not an object for an 'I think', it is a grouping of lived-through meanings which moves towards its equilibrium." (*Phenomenology of Perception* 153). I am my body and this embodied consciousness that I am extends beyond my body proper. The body-subject extends to the car that I drive, the musical instrument I play, or the cane I use if I am blind. These instruments become extensions of my body and as I move around the world, I apprehend the world with them, I understand it with them. Their status is the same as that of my limbs and they serve the same function for me. While I am driving, I am one with the car I drive. My body encompasses the vehicle and I am in the world as a consciousness-driving-a-car.

What then is the ego, and how is it formed? The "I" is transcendent, it is in the world and as vulnerable as other objects in the world. Sartre explains: "Instead of expressing itself in effect as 'I alone exist as absolute,' it must assert that 'absolute consciousness alone exists as absolute,' which is obviously a truism. My *I*, in effect, is *no more certain for consciousness than the I of other men*. It is only more intimate" (TE 104). The I and the world are objects for consciousness. The I is not the core of our being, consciousness is and it creates an ego for itself.

This is quite a revision of Descartes' and Husserl's positions! The ego is evicted from consciousness; it is merely an object. In that sense, then, I can intend my ego and create it as I make it an object for me. The difference between the "me" and other objects is that objects are already there, outside myself, whereas the "me" is dependent on me. What is really important is that "[i]f the Ego and the world are both objects of consciousness, if neither has created the other, then consciousness, by establishing the relations between them, insures the active participation of the person in the world." (Barnes xiv).

Also important to note is the relation that is established between consciousness and the world. The "world" is what consciousness makes it. We create a world on the basis of what we encounter "out there," i.e. outside of ourselves. We give meaning to what we meet, and we thus make the world our own. The ego is also born of this encounter: I make myself, and I make the world as I go about it and act in view of my project. We will see this in more detail in Chapter 3.

THE REFUSAL OF THE UNCONSCIOUS

Note that there is a very famous twentieth-century character missing from this picture: the unconscious. Sartre refused, denied, fought against this Freudian feature. Sartre was horrified by the thought that there could be a part of ourselves that would not be conscious. Since we are consciousness, there cannot be such a thing as an un-consciousness; un-consciousness would be the same as un-existence to Sartre.

SIGMUND FREUD

Psychoanalyst Sigmund Freud (1856–1939) presented a view of human subjectivity as a tripartite system: the id, the ego, and the superego. Trying to understand how neuroses come to be (i.e. how one can behave in a "non-rational" way) Freud posits a complex inner-working of consciousness. The ego is our "rational" part, the one that acts and that has daily experiences. The superego is an internalization of rules (the rule of the father, society's rules, etc.). The id, the unconscious, is that part of our psyche in which we store traumatic events in an effort to repress them and to erase them from our consciousness. The repressed parts of our psyche are responsible not only for deviant behaviour, such as neuroses and psychoses, but also for much of our daily actions. In fact, for Freud, the ego seems pretty powerless faced with the superego and the id. Importantly too, he ascribes to the unconscious a major role in our psychic life, something inconceivable for Sartre, for whom to exist is to be conscious.

Interestingly, it is not against Freud that he first argues the unconscious away. Rather, in *The Transcendence of the Ego*, his target is French moralist François, duc de La Rochefoucauld (1613–80), one of the first to have made use of the concept of the unconscious. In his commentary on the essay, Vincent de Coorebyter explains that, at the time, Sartre did not feel secure enough in his knowledge of Freud's theory to engage in a sustained criticism of his views on the unconscious (see de Coorebyter's edition of *La Transcendance de L'Ego*, 2003: 186–7). So his criticism is directed at psychologists, like La Rochefoucauld, who confuse the pre-reflective mode of consciousness with a reflective mode that would not be conscious. The example Sartre uses to demonstrate this is that of Pierre-having-to-be-helped. I find Pierre to be in need of help and, pitying him, I help him out. The quality of "having-to-be-helped" is a quality of Pierre himself, and not an element of an unconscious part of our psyche that would trigger my response of helping Pierre. There is no unconscious "drive" as such that pushes me to help Pierre; rather it is Pierre as "having-to-be-helped" that drives me into action. One may try to explain my deed by saying that I had an unconscious drive to eliminate an unpleasurable feeling at the sight of Pierre's misery, but, to Sartre, this is ignoring that there is an objective fact concerning Pierre's situation (of being endangered and in need of help), and that it is this objective fact, external to consciousness, that my consciousness responds to. There is no trick, no mysterious doer or motivation. Pierre-having-to-be-helped is out there in the world, my consciousness encounters him and responds by helping.

This important denial of the unconscious is further argued for in *Being and Nothingness*. Sartre is adamant to show that to exist is to be conscious and that there is no unconscious. In *Being and Nothingness*, he argues against the unconscious by appealing to the concept of bad faith. With this, he explains that it is quite possible for an individual to lie to himself about himself without making use of an unconscious (we will discuss this in Chapter 4). The rejection of the unconscious will also play a role when Sartre later says that man is entirely responsible for himself: if there existed an unconscious, responsibility might be attributed to it (which is what he sees at work in psychoanalysis, for example), and the individual would thus not be entirely responsible. We will discuss this in more details in Chapter 3.

IMAGINATION AND EMOTION

As we have seen so far, Sartre's approach to the nature of consciousness and what it means to be a conscious being implies a substantial revision of traditional views. Most importantly, it deepens the Cartesian view in proposing that consciousness is multi-layered, and at the same time it refutes the psychoanalytic approach that speaks of unconscious processes. Sartre's views of consciousness are also made more complex as he tackles the notions of imagination and emotions. These problems are interesting to scrutinize for any philosopher because they are so distinctly human. Imagination, for example, points to a capacity of the human being to create objects for itself—objects that do not already have an existence in the world.

What is peculiar in Sartre's approach is that he presents imagination and emotions as ways for consciousness to exist in the world. Imagination is not a tool for consciousness; rather, it is a way for consciousness to be in the world, as "imaginative consciousness." Imagination is dependent on the world, insofar as the images that we form are always somehow related to the experience we have had of them. However, a close examination of imagination reveals that it is in fact the pure expression of the freedom of consciousness. In order to be able to imagine, imagination has to synthesize the world into a unity, and then must negate this world. As imaginative consciousness, it goes beyond and negates this world of the real. In order to form an "un-real" object, an imagined object, the imaginative consciousness must constitute the world as a unity aside from itself and must go beyond it. In order to imagine a make-believe object named "Zyptrod," my consciousness has first to consolidate what it knows about the world. It then negates the world as one where there are no Zyptrods. The Zyptrod my consciousness then posits is an unreal object. It is the pure outcome of an entirely free act of creation by my consciousness. It depends on the world only insofar as I need to negate the world, to go beyond it.

Sartre claims that there is no other universe than that of human subjectivity, but he also says that "if you were to take the world away from consciousness, it would no longer be consciousness of anything, therefore no longer consciousness at all" (Notebooks 558). Consciousness is always consciousness *of* something. In order to explore these ideas differently, Sartre examines how a human being would react if this process was disrupted. What if a human being could see the world as it really is, i.e. as it is before consciousness intends it? And similarly, how would such a being experience himself as consciousness? These questions are put forth in Sartre's important philosophical novel, *Nausea*.

ROQUENTIN'S NAUSEA

The novel, published in 1938 but written at the same time as *The Transcendence of the Ego*, is the journal of Antoine Roquentin, the fictional main character. A note to the reader opens the novel, in which the fictional editors explain that they are merely reproducing the notebooks they found in the papers of Antoine Roquentin. They are his journal, written while he was doing research for his history book on the Marquis de Rollebon at the library of Bouville. In his journal, Roquentin notes that his relationship with the world, with things, and with people has profoundly changed. He is trying to understand what has happened, as he is experiencing a heretofore unknown feeling of disgust toward things. What initially triggered the nausea was when he grasped a pellet to throw it in the water:

> Ever since the day I wanted to play ducks and drakes. I was going to throw that pebble, I looked at it and then it all began: I felt that it *existed*. Then after that there were other Nauseas; from time to time objects start existing in your hand.

(N 122–3)

Roquentin's relationship with the world is disturbed as existence reveals its very self to him. Using language, Roquentin tries to make sense of his experience of existing. He has discovered that he exists, that he is surrounded by existence, and yet he cannot name things or make sense of them. He says: "Things are divorced from their names." (N 125).

The episode of the park is most telling of his encounter with existence. Roquentin goes to the park in Bouville and sits on a bench under which the roots of a chesnut tree are sunk into the ground. Roquentin has a vision that leaves him breathless. He says:

> Existence had suddenly unveiled itself. It had lost the harmless look of an abstract category: […] the root, the park gates, the bench, the sparse grass, all that had vanished: the diversity of things, their individuality, were only an appearance, a veneer. This veneer had melted, leaving soft, monstrous masses, all in disorder – naked, in a frightful, obscene nakedness.
>
> (N 127)

As he goes on in his astonishment, he explains how this world resists language, resists meaning: "the world of explanations and reasons is not the world of existence. […] This root […] existed in such a way that I could not explain it" (N 129). The encounter with existence goes further as Roquentin explains that "I *was* the root of the chestnut tree. Or rather I was entirely conscious of its existence. Still detached from it — since I was conscious of it — yet lost in it, nothing but it" (N 131). We will revisit this passage in the next chapter.

NAUSEA AND THE UNDERGROUND MAN

Written in 1864 while he was sitting at the deathbed of his first wife, Russian novelist Fyodor Dostoevsky's (1821–81) *Notes from the Underground* present us with a peculiar character who can be said to grasp existence without its veneer. The ramblings of his character allow him to expose his view of consciousness and unconsciousness. He rejects the view according to which the human being is one and indivisible: this to him is a fiction. The human being is a multiplicity, he is not the expression of an essence, he is pure existence, and this life, as we get to know from reading the *Notes*, is more than the life of reason. This brings him close to Roquentin's own realization in *Nausea*.

It is quite interesting to read this passage in light of the developments that Sartre makes on the pre-reflective consciousness in the essay *Transcendence of the Ego*, wherein he makes the Husserlian notion of intentionality his own. When Roquentin exclaims, "I *was* the root," he is expressing a phenomenological truth. As an intentional consciousness that is not personal, he literally is the root as he experiences it. In the pre-reflective mode of consciousness, there is no "I" that can claim to be having the experience. All that there is, is the experience itself. The reason why Roquentin suffers from nausea is because the boundaries between things and the self are blurred as existence reveals itself to him in its "gross nakedness." This is what leads Roquentin to declare, despite the fact that he knows he exists: "Now when I say 'I,' it seems hollow to me. I can't manage to feel myself very well, I am so forgotten. The only real thing left in me is existence which feels it exists" (N 170). There is consciousness as conscious *of* something. There is no ego maneuvering in the world. All there is, is "consciousness of all that and consciousness of consciousness" (N 171). Roquentin has lost his "I," although it remains a constant possibility for him. When he meets with other people, his consciousness is individuated again, his ego re-emerges.

Nausea is thus experienced as a loss of meaning on different levels. The world loses meaning as things begin to exist and lose the veneer that human reason has put on them. We will discuss this in further details in the following chapter. The individual existence also loses meaning as one experiences the loss of one's self. Roquentin's ego becomes a fleeting, evanescent thing. What he considered to be the core of his being is now merely a little part of his self. He uncovers the inner workings of his consciousness. He also obscurely senses his consciousness as pre-reflective.

Nausea is the state that Roquentin is in while he fails to see meaning in the world or in himself. To actually experience oneself as not a self is a scary and nauseating experience for the individual. However, we do not experience ourselves like that; rather we live by the illusion that we are a simple unified being. This is probably helpful to us in the long run, as it helps us to get by from day to day. For his part, the philosopher needs to understand what lies behind that veneer. For Sartre, it is, as we have seen, the multi-layered consciousness that creates an ego for itself as it interacts with the world. In the following chapter, we will see how the encounter between consciousness and being happens: Sartre distinguishes between two types of beings, and the encounter between the two generates the human world.

SUMMARY

Sartre's views clearly present a revision of the Cartesian rationalistic view of the subject as a *cogito*. They also present an inversion of the Husserlian view, insofar as the ego is an object in the world and not the unity of my perceptions of the world. In *The Transcendence of the Ego*, he explains that the I, the ego, the subject of the Cartesian "I think," is really a by-product of the involvement of consciousness in the world. The "I" becomes an object of consciousness, just like any other object in the world. It is not the core of the human being. It is an object in the world, just like any other object, only more intimate. Consciousness is more fundamental, and lies at the root of the world. It creates the world by giving meaning to what it encounters outside of itself, as an intentional consciousness, i.e. as conscious *of* something. Therefore, Sartre suggests that we must replace Descartes' formula "I think, therefore I am" with "There is consciousness, therefore I am." In Descartes, the "therefore" seemed superfluous, since to affirm one's thinking being meant to affirm one's existence. "I think" translates into "I am." However, in Sartre, the "therefore" literally conveys how the ego emerges: consciousness is first and absolute, and then the "I" emerges later. It is because there is consciousness as conscious *of* that the "I" can exist.

2

BEING

In the preceding chapter, we examined Sartre's phenomenology. Sartre's views on consciousness allowed him to reject traditional rationalistic views, which he considered reductive of the human experience. Now that we understand the phenomenological positions related to consciousness, we can now turn our attention to Sartre's ontology, i.e. his theory of being, as he exposes it in his *magnum opus*, *Being and Nothingness*. His aim is to provide the reader with as complete a description as possible of being, using the phenomenological views that he exposed earlier in *The Transcendence of the Ego*. Sartre claims—many times—that his project is not metaphysical in nature. By this, he means that he is not looking for a justification of existence or some sort of explanation as to why being is rather than not—an explanation that would lie beyond this world and this existence for metaphysics. Instead, he dismisses such questions by insisting on the fundamental contingency of everything that exists. Even his starting point, the human being, is purely contingent, gratuitous, *de trop*. In *Nausea*, Roquentin's discovery of this state of affairs is partly responsible for his sickness. If an explanation of the existence of beings, and human beings in particular, is thus not Sartre's concern—for there is no such explanation—it remains that a description of being and its different modes is both possible and necessary.

In this chapter, we will begin by examining Sartre's definition of being. We will see how he distinguishes being from human being. We will then discuss some particularities of the human being, such as contingency, facticity, and the situated body. This will be followed by a brief consideration of the notion of transcendence (which will be further fleshed out in Chapter 3), which will lead us to discuss Sartre's atheism and his rejection of transcendent realms.

BEING IN-ITSELF

Sartre begins his treatise by indicating his rejection of any dualistic view of the world. Dualism conceives of the world as composed of two different realms. For example, Plato thought that the world we live in is an imperfect copy of the perfect world of Forms. He thought these two worlds were separate, distinct realms of being. Another example of dualism can be found in the philosophy of Descartes (discussed earlier), insofar as he regards the realms of mind and matter to be incommensurable. For his part, Sartre wants to present a view in which there are different modes of being instead of different realms of being, i.e. that there are different ways for being to be. The two most fundamental modes in Sartre's ontology are being in-itself and being for-itself. With regards to being in-itself, we cannot say more than that the "in-itself is," because the in-itself lies beyond our experience of it, our being conscious of it. While consciousness is conscious (of) being, it does not reach being; rather it encounters a phenomenon of its own making. What is unveiled through our conscious grasp of being is a world supported by being, of which we can say nothing but that it *is*. Remember that we have seen with the concept of intentionality in Chapter 1 that consciousness taints what it perceives and thus it creates its own world. Being in-itself is thus said to be transphenomenal, i.e. it lies beyond the phenomenal experience of humans. This is why Sartre defines ontology as "the description of the phenomenon of being as it manifests itself" (BN 7). All the human being can hope to describe is this being *as* phenomenon, and not the being in-itself that lies beyond it, beyond our experience. The ontological inquiry presented by Sartre in *Being and Nothingness* is thus tainted by the intentionality of consciousness presented in earlier works (we have examined those in Chapter 1). It must, therefore, be a "phenomenological ontology."

Given this, all one can say is: "Being is. Being is in-itself. Being is what it is" (BN 29). This definition allows us to infer a few things about being. First, being in-itself is full of itself; it is a fullness of being without any lack. The world of differences, categories, objects, space, and time is the world of phenomena for consciousness. It is consciousness that introduces such distinctions, and thus generates a world. Being in-itself, however, remains unaffected by this. It is what it is. It is timeless, changeless: it is.

How does Sartre determine the existence of being in-itself when all we have access to as intentional consciousnesses are phenomena? As he explains, the fact that these phenomena happen is sufficient proof that there is an in-itself. Refuting Berkeley's idealist view that "to be is to be perceived," Sartre takes the appearance of phenomena as an indication that there is a being in-itself behind it. Further, the very nature of consciousness is taken as a proof that there exists an in-itself. Consciousness exists only as conscious *of* something. As such, there has to be a being of which it can be conscious in order for it to exist. Sartre says: "If you were to take the world away from consciousness, it would no longer be consciousness of anything, therefore no longer consciousness at all" (Notebooks 558). Sartre will eventually refute the charge that his conception of being is dualistic, saying that being for-itself exists only because there is a being in-itself. They are intertwined and necessitate each other.

BERKELEY'S *ESSE EST PERCIPI*

The Irish bishop George Berkeley (1685–1753) was a metaphysical idealist. He held that reality is mental in nature. For an object to exist, it has to exist as sense data in our minds, hence his famous statement: "To be is to be perceived or to be a perceiver." Human beings exist as minds that perceive, and objects exist in these minds only as perceived, i.e. as collections of sense data. God is the ultimate cause of the sense perceptions that we have in our minds, and God is the ultimate perceiver. All that exists substantially are minds, human and godly. This differs significantly from Sartre's view in two important ways: first, that there is material substance as well as mental substance for Sartre; second, Sartre's philosophy is atheistic.

BEING FOR-ITSELF

In contrast to being in-itself, being for-itself is the being that "is what it is not and is not what it is." This famous Sartrean formula, repeated many times throughout the treatise, summarizes what the existence of consciousness is. Being for-itself is the mode of being of consciousness, i.e. of the human being. The human being is in the mode of the for-itself. When Sartre uses the term "for-itself," he is referring to the human being. He says that the for-itself is none other than the nothingness that encounters Being. The for-itself, the human being, i.e. consciousness, is conceived of as a nothingness of Being, as a lack of Being. Indeed, intentional consciousness is initially empty, a void that is filled through its consciousness (of) the world (see the analysis of this in Chapter 1). An emptiness, a nothingness, consciousness is that by which negation comes to the world. However, in its encounter with Being, consciousness can introduce negations such as absence. It is only for a consciousness that something is said to be missing, to lack, to not exist. Sartre's example of the quarter moon is telling. It can be said to be "merely" a quarter only when a consciousness expects a full moon. But the moon as quarter moon exists fully as what it is; it is only for consciousness that it is lacking in any way.

PIERRE'S ABSENCE

In *Being and Nothingness*, a flurry of examples are used by Sartre to illustrate his theories. A recurrent character is Pierre. To explain how consciousness introduces negation into the world, he considers the example of Pierre's "absence" in the café. It is only if I come to the café with an expectation to see Pierre that I can notice his absence (his non-presence) if he is not there. However, as Sartre insists, the café and its crowd is a fullness of presence to me. It is with this background and due to my expectation to find Pierre that I can say, "Pierre is not here, he is absent." In-itself, there is only a fullness of being to be found in the café.

Because consciousness is this nothingness, which introduces negation in the world, the for-itself comes to be defined as the being that has to be what it is not. It is not fully itself, and this distance from itself allows it to form projects as well as to be free from determinations, i.e. to move ahead in the future as what it is not, by denying the past. It is freedom that allows us to back away from the fullness of being. As Sartre says: "Freedom is the human being putting his past out of play by secreting his own nothingness" (BN 64). Indeed, as a free being, my possibilities are merely possible; nothing binds me to them. I am not what I am, and even though I can form an image of what I wish to be but am not, nothing determines me to accomplish it (we will discuss this in more detail in Chapter 3). It is for this reason that Sartre refers to the free human being as a set of possibles.

THE GAMBLER

The gambler who decided yesterday that he would no longer gamble realizes in anguish that he has to reiterate his decision of not gambling at every moment. He is not bound by his past decision. If confronted with the decision of whether or not to gamble *now*, he must, in the present, decide (again) that he will not gamble. His present decision is absolutely free and his future being is absolutely undetermined, even by his present decision to gamble or not. He will, in the future, as in the now, have to decide again. Thus freedom can be anguishing as the for-itself realizes that there is a separation between "me" and my "self" as an essence. As Sartre would say, "Essence is all that human reality apprehends in itself as having been. It is here that anguish appears as an apprehension of self inasmuch as it exists in the perpetual mode of detachment from what is […]" (BN 72–3). We will discuss this again in Chapter 4.

The for-itself is a being in a situation that has a certain grasp on the world and shapes itself through it. Sartre says that the for-itself is a project; it is constantly making itself. Being a nothingness and a nihilating being, the for-itself is not determined, and is hence free to become through its actions. It can freely break from its past or even from social or historical conditioning, and affirm itself through its actions. This freedom that the for-itself has, however, generates anguish, an anguish that is so powerful that one will be tempted to flee it by engaging in bad faith (see Chapter 4).

CONTINGENCY AND FACTICITY

The for-itself is in a somewhat "tragic" situation. It exists, and yet there is no reason for it to exist. The for-itself is thus a contingent being in a world of facticity. Sartre defines facticity by saying that "while it is necessary that I be in the form of being-there, still it is altogether contingent that I be, for I am not the foundation of my being" (BN 407). Further, there is no reason for me to be engaged in the world in that particular situation rather than in another. These are contingent facts about human beings.

The most vivid descriptions of the contingency of Being, and how the human being tackles it, are to be found in Sartre's 1938 novel *Nausea*. The main protagonist, Antoine Roquentin, is struggling with bouts of nausea. When he suffers from it, things lose their meaning, the world loses its veneer and he can see existence itself: the world as a "gross, absurd being" (we discussed this in Chapter 1). One afternoon he sits in the park of Bouville and lets himself be fascinated by the root of a chestnut tree. The experience leaves him speechless, and it is only later, back in his room while writing in his journal, that he can explain what happened and put his discovery into words:

> The essential thing is contingency. I mean that one cannot define existence as necessity. To exist is simply *to be there*; those who exist let themselves be encountered, but you can never deduce anything from them. I believe there are people who have understood this. Only they tried to overcome this contingency by inventing a necessary, causal being. But no necessary being can explain existence: contingency is not a delusion, a probability which can be dissipated; it is the absolute, consequently, the perfect free gift. All is gratuitous, this park, this city and myself. When you realize that, it turns your heart upside down and everything begins to float […]
>
> (N 131, translation altered)

To discover that everything, including oneself, is gratuitous, i.e. superfluous, that there is no reason to be there or not, leads Roquentin to his nauseating experience. Peter Caws explains:

> Nausea and boredom are what Sartre calls "primordial reactions" (*réactions originelles*); they mark the most fundamental relationship of consciousness with being, on what has come to be called the "visceral level". While however they remind us forcefully of the existence of Being-in-itself, they tell us nothing whatever about it; […]
>
> (Caws *Sartre* 96)

It is this experience of not being told anything about being in-itself, yet being reminded of its existence, that leads Roquentin to his furious outburst:

I was not surprised, I knew it was the World, the naked World suddenly revealing itself, and I choked with rage at this gross, absurd being. You couldn't even wonder where all that sprang from, or how it was that a world came into existence, rather than nothingness. It didn't make sense, the World was everywhere, in front, behind. There had been nothing *before* it. Nothing. There had never been a moment in which it could not have existed. That was what worried me: of course there was no reason for this flowing lava to exist. But it was impossible for it not to exist. It was unthinkable: to imagine nothingness you had to be there already, in the midst of the World, eyes wide open and alive; nothingness was only an idea in my head, an existing idea floating in this immensity: this nothingness had not come before existence, it was an existence like any other and appeared after many others. I shouted "filth! what rotten filth!" and shook myself to get rid of this sticky filth, but it held fast and there was so much, tons and tons of existence, endless: I stifled at the depths of this immense weariness. And then suddenly the park emptied as through a great hole, the World disappeared as it had come, or else I woke up—in any case, I saw no more of it; nothing was left but the yellow earth around me, out of which dead branches rose upward.

(N 134–5)

Roquentin has uncovered the reality of being as well as its pure contingency. There is no reason for it to be there. Being in-itself is also out of our reach. What we experience, if we are not suffering from nausea, is the world as meaningful. Being in-itself has no meaning and has no place for the human being: it is indifferent to him. On Sartre's view, this is what constitutes our superfluity, our gratuitousness. The human being's existence is entirely contingent and this is why he constantly needs to be justified: from the point of view of Being, his existence is not necessary. We will revisit these ideas in Chapter 6.

Roquentin is suffering from an inner need for a justification of existence, a need that will always remain unsatisfied. Sartre thinks that the human being is constantly seeking explanations and reasons. We have what Nietzsche would call a metaphysical instinct.

FRIEDRICH NIETZSCHE'S CRITIQUE OF METAPHYSICS

The German philosopher Friedrich Nietzsche (1844–1900) was a very influential figure for twentieth-century philosophy, and for the existentialist movement in particular. He is the first philosopher to be mentioned by name in *Being and Nothingness*, in which Sartre expresses his agreement with the Nietzschean critique of metaphysics. Nietzsche thought that human beings have a need for explanations, and that they constantly seek to give meaning to their lives. When no meaning is found, they invent discourses to satisfy their own need. This is the origin of metaphysical discourse, on Nietzsche's account. However, human beings start to believe in the truth of their own inventions, and forget that they were the ones to create these discourses to satisfy their needs. Metaphysical discourses that erect a reality behind appearances, a reality that is held to be truer than the one experienced by humans, are alienating for human beings. One of Nietzsche's major targets is the metaphysics of Plato. Plato puts in place a world of Forms. The human world is the world of appearances, i.e. a world composed of copies of the real objects which are the Forms. The world is thus divided between the transcendent world of Forms—both more true and more real—and the immanent human world, an imperfect copy of the true world. Nietzsche believes that in such a setting the human will disregard his own self and his own immanent well-being in favor of a world beyond, which does not in fact exist. The metaphysical view offers an answer to the "Why" of existence, but deprives human experiences of their quality by the same token. Nietzsche says that we must free ourselves of such alienating discourses, and Sartre agrees.

When we seek meaning for being and for our own existence, we are looking for an a priori meaning. We forget that we are the beings through which meaning comes to the world in the first place. Being in-itself is devoid of meaning; it simply *is*. The presence of the for-itself generates meaning for Being. Intentional consciousness is thus an interpretive consciousness. We live in the world, not in the in-itself, and the world is a meaningful place (see Chapter 1). The meaning is a human meaning and not an a priori meaning. In the conclusion of *Being and Nothingness*, Sartre explains that it makes no sense to ask why there is Being, since Being is needed in the first place, in order to articulate the question. One would have to engage in metaphysics to attempt a response, and Sartre refuses to. We simply have to come to terms with the fact that we are contingent beings. We have to assume our facticity in all of its aspects.

My facticity encompasses the contingent fact of my presence in the world, as well as the particularities of that presence: this body that I am, the situation that I am engaged in, this family, this social class, this skin color, this gender, etc. The fact of human freedom is also part of facticity. I cannot help but be a free being. "We are condemned to be free" is one of the most famous Sartrean statements, and yet one of the most inexplicable. The for-itself exists as a free consciousness engaged in the world via its body. There is no overarching reason for this to be the case, no justification for this fact. We are simply free beings and have to assume the responsibility for this. Hence, freedom is also constitutive of my facticity.

THE SITUATED BODY

The for-itself is a situated, embodied being. Consciousness is engaged in the world via the body that it is. Recall that some rationalist philosophers, like Descartes, conceived of the mind as being in control of the body, in the same way that a hand may use an instrument. The body was conceived to be a tool for the mind to accomplish what it wants. Sartre's view is very different. When discussing the relationship between consciousness and the body, Sartre attempts to avoid presenting a dualistic view where the two would be conceived as separate parts of the whole being that the for-itself is. He will thus say that we are both entirely body *and* consciousness. For the human being, to be is to exist as a body in a world of objects. Sartre insists that our starting point must be our being-in-the-world rather than our soul. We have to keep in mind that consciousness, which appears to be the first fact, is in fact conscious (of), and that in order for it to exist, it must be in the world; it can only be conscious by having experiences as embodied. The body is, as Sartre says, "the contingent form which is assumed by the necessity of my contingency" (BN 408). It is necessary that I have a body, but it is contingent that I have that particular body.

The body is my situation and it is my contingency. It is through my body that the world arises for me. However, Sartre refuses to make a mere instrument of it. It is an instrument insofar as I use it as my point of insertion in being, as the point of upsurge for my world. It is the center of action for the for-itself. When I go about the world, I articulate it by my use of objects and by my actions. The hand that I "use" is not an instrument but an act. My hand is the meaning and orientation of the range of instruments that constitute my world. The center of the complex is the instrument that I am. The body is lived:

> Far from the body being first *for us* and revealing things to us, it is the instrumental-things which in their original appearance indicate our body to us. The body is not a screen between things and ourselves; it manifests only the individuality and the contingency of our original relation to instrumental-things.
>
> (BN 428–9)

Action is the being-in-the-world of the for-itself. The body is the immediate presence of the for-itself to things as action. I am my body at the same time as I am not it. I am it as the starting point of my action and I am not it as I can surpass it by my action.

My consciousness exists as its body: it is embodied. Sartre discusses the example of eye-pain to strengthen his view on embodiment. If I am reading while experiencing eye-pain, my whole experience of the world and of myself as conscious (of) is tainted by the pain in my eyes. I become a painful consciousness. While I can focus my attention on my act of reading or on my body, my painful eyes, the pain of my body is lived—it is my lived consciousness. Thus it is contingent that I have this body rather than another, but it is necessary that I have a body and the body that I have makes me the consciousness that I am. This constitutes another important aspect of my facticity. However, Sartre also presents the for-itself as a being that is not absolutely bound by its facticity. The for-itself, as freedom, can transcend itself: it can surpass its facticity.

TRANSCENDENCE

Given that the for-itself is a nothingness, that it is what it is not and is not what it is, it can transcend itself. In fact, it cannot help but transcend itself. Every relation that the for-itself is engaged in is an act of transcendence, i.e. a movement outside of oneself. The case Sartre examines is that of knowledge, for "it is the very being of the for-itself in so far as this is presence to—" (BN 242). As an intentional consciousness that is conscious (of), the for-itself is present to the in-itself. This is not a reciprocal relationship, as being in-itself cannot "respond" to that presence. When I know something, my consciousness is present to the thing known. I am present to what I am not, i.e. the known thing is not me. This relationship between the for-itself and the in-itself, which is a fundamental one, shows that the for-itself is constantly outside itself, that it constitutes itself via this movement outside of oneself. It is this aspect of its being that allows it to be a project, i.e. to make itself. In that sense, transcendence is constitutive of the for-itself. We will reexamine this idea in further detail in Chapter 3.

SARTRE'S ATHEISM AND REJECTION OF TRANSCENDENT REALMS

The transcendence that Sartre talks about is an "immanent" one—a strictly human one. One can speak of transcendence only in relation to the for-itself that is a project or that can transcend objects of its consciousness. For Sartre, there are no transcendent realms beyond this world. The world is human, i.e. the fruit of the encounter between consciousness and being. Being in-itself, which is out of reach for consciousness, is still conceived of as this-worldly. It certainly is not the equivalent of a world of Forms as we find in Plato. There is no reality beyond this reality. The only reality is a human one. There are no transcendent realms of being. We dwell in Being, and there is no world beyond Being.

This position entails an atheism that Sartre has repeatedly claimed. However, it is not clear whether it is this ontological position that guides his adoption of atheism. Rather, it seems that his lack of faith corresponds neatly with an ontological view that excludes transcendent beings such as God.

SARTRE AND GOD: AN EARLY ATHEISM

Sartre's atheism is both the result of a personal experience that he had in his youth, and the logical conclusion of his philosophical positions. In *Words*, he tells the story of how, aged 12 in 1917, he discovered with a "polite astonishment" that God did not exist. Waiting for friends on his way to school in La Rochelle and looking for something to occupy his mind, he mused about God. As he did, "He [God] at once stumbled down into the blue sky and vanished without explanation: He does not exist, I said to myself [...] and I thought the matter settled." (Words 170). In his *Entretiens* with Simone de Beauvoir in 1974, he admits that—although he devised fancy arguments for atheism—in fact his own reasons for not believing in God were not really philosophical.

In his public lecture *Existentialism is a Humanism*, Sartre provides an argument to support atheism. Existentialism takes human subjectivity as its starting point. There is no universe other than a human universe. Given that, there is nothing that can exist outside of that universe, and all that exists in that universe exists for the human. This is what the circuit of selfness explains. As an intentional consciousness, I constitute a world for me; whatever lies outside of my world literally does not exist for me. God, as an all-powerful, eternal, spiritual, and transcendent being has no place in this. Given that there is no God, the human being does not have an essence. "Existence precedes essence" for the human being, because no almighty being has given or determined an essence for the human being. The human being is left to himself—"abandoned" as Sartre says, but free.

Sartre considers the death of God as a genuine liberation for human beings, as expressed in the play *The Devil and the Good Lord*. Goetz, the main protagonist, who undergoes much spiritual transformation in the play, embraces belief in God for a while. He wants to be good and tries his best to be a good believer. However, his attempt fails. He comes to the conclusion that God does not exist, and declares:

Each minute I wondered what I could *be* in the eyes of God. Now I know the answer: nothing. God does not see me, God does not hear me, God does not know me. You see this emptiness over our heads? That is God.

(Devil 141)

Goetz—and Sartre—consider this a liberation for the human being: "He doesn't exist [...] I have delivered us. No more Heaven, no more Hell; nothing but Earth" (Devil 141–2). It is a true liberation, but it is, at the same time, a condemnation to freedom. If there is no God, we are entirely responsible for what we make of ourselves. We are left without any excuses.

Sartre has said that the death of God is the equivalent to the death of all transcendence, but with it comes "the opening of the infinite" (Notebooks 34), i.e. the infinite of human possibilities. As he puts it in his *Notebooks for an Ethics*, "In this way, man finds himself the heir of the mission of the dead God: to draw Being from its perpetual collapse into the absolute indistinctness of night. An infinite mission" (Notebooks 494). His atheism results in a loss of meaning, a meaning that the human being will have to create anew in the wake of God's death and the absence of any transcendent being. The human being is up for the task, as a for-itself that is an intentional consciousness embodied in a situation. As such, he creates the world by giving meaning to the in-itself. As we will see in the following chapter, the for-itself is also conceived as fundamentally free. As such, he or she has to create values for him or herself. Atheism and the rejection of transcendent realms makes room for that freedom which Sartre will consider to be absolute.

SUMMARY

Sartre describes two modes of being: being in-itself and being for-itself. Being in-itself is a fullness of being, while being for-itself is being that is conscious of itself, i.e. human consciousness or, as Sartre would have it, the nothingness that encounters Being (hence the treatise's title). It is that which introduces negation in the world. The for-itself is shown to be a factical and contingent being. The human being is thrown into the world. There is no reason for individuals to exist, nor is there an explanation for the existence of the world. They are simply there. The contingent human being is defined as a free, situated, embodied consciousness. Because the for-itself is free, it is a transcendent being that can surpass its facticity. The Sartrean ontological set-up excludes traditional forms of transcendence, and the one it admits is an immanent one. There is no room for transcendent realms or God in Sartre's philosophy, which thus presents itself as necessarily atheistic.

3

FREEDOM

In the last chapter, we touched upon a very important aspect of Sartre's philosophy, namely the idea that the human being makes him/herself. The individual surpasses herself towards some goals and thus exerts her own transcendence. The human being is a project. What allows the human being to make him/herself is the fact that he is fundamentally free. It is to the notion of Sartrean freedom that this chapter is devoted. Many readers of Sartre are initially shocked by his view that the individual is absolutely free and absolutely responsible. Taking this literally, they believe that Sartre means that one is always free to do whatever one wants. Readers often confuse Sartre's notion of freedom with the freedom of acting whimsically upon any desire or the capacity to achieve whatever one wishes. It would be shocking if he did claim that. However, when Sartre claims that we are absolutely free, his claim stems not only from his ontology but also from his atheistic position. There is no God who decides for us and imposes values on us; accordingly, we must create our own values. As beings that are free, we can do that—but we must be ready to accept the consequences. Indeed, for Sartre, freedom is not merely a license to act whimsically; it entails responsibility. One is free but one is also entirely responsible for one's own freedom. Again, it is in *Being and Nothingness* that we find the theoretical basis for such a view. After all, Sartre has referred to his *magnum opus* as being a "treatise on freedom." So in this chapter, we will first examine the concept of freedom as exposed in *Being and Nothingness* and in literary texts. I will then explain what absolute responsibility is. Following this, we will address the notion of project that has been exposed very briefly in the preceding chapter. This will be the occasion to explain the Sartrean phrase "existence precedes essence." We will also examine how Sartre explores the intricacies of freedom and responsibility in his plays and novels.

THE SITUATION

In Chapter 2, we have said that consciousness is not what it is: it has to be what it is not. It is a presence to oneself, but this presence is constantly in the making. Consciousness never really corresponds to itself. It is never what it is: it is temporal and it is free, so always in the making. As it exists, the for-itself surpasses its past and its situation. It is a project, i.e. a being that has a past as an essence but that is always transcending that past.

> It is never what it is. What it is is behind it as the perpetual surpassed. It is precisely this surpassed facticity which we call the Past. The Past then is a necessary structure of the For-itself; for the For-itself can exist only as a nihilating surpassing, and this surpassing implies something surpassed.
>
> (BN 197)

The past is thus the "in-itself" of the present. It is a determination of my being, since I have a past and carry it with me but, at the same time, I surpass it. I am not bound to it; I make myself with and despite my past.

In addition to surpassing one's past, the human being is also transcending a situation that is constituted by the body, the family, the social class, the country, the ethnicity, etc. The situation is the material objective set of the human being's life. It is something that we cannot avoid, change, or get rid of. The for-itself is a being-in-situation. But this being-in-situation is a being that constantly acts upon his situation. This is the action of the for-itself as project. Sartre describes this as the paradox of freedom: "There is freedom only in a situation, and there is a situation only through freedom" (BN 629). Indeed, since consciousness is freedom, freedom is in a situation. Remember what we said of the embodied consciousness in Chapter 2. Consciousness is in a body, and this body is its anchoring point in the world. It is its point of view on the world. Minimally then, I am situated in that point of view that my body is. My body is also located in the world: it is in a family, a social class, a country, a historical period, etc. There is an objective aspect of the situation: I cannot help but be born in this female body, in a working-class family, in Canada, in the twentieth century. However, it is I who determine the meaning of this situation. This is what allows Sartre to say that the situation exists through freedom: my free consciousness gives meaning to that situation in which I am born. By doing so, I am in a position to transcend and surpass my situation. My situation is thus not entirely determining of my being.

THE FUNDAMENTAL PROJECT

So to Sartre, we are determined by our situation only insofar as we let ourselves be determined by it. Sartre defines the for-itself as a project. This is the inner structure that we find in the human being of "throwing itself" into a future. "I am nothing but the project of myself beyond a determined situation, and this project *pre-outlines* me in terms of the concrete situation as in addition it illumines the situation in terms of my choice" (BN 706). Being a project, the for-itself is always transcending his/her own situation by making use of his own freedom. His situation is the starting-point, the springboard toward another future situation. We should be careful here, however: to say that the for-itself is a project is not the same as to say that the for-itself *has* projects. I may be planning a vacation for this summer. This is a single project I have. But it does not constitute myself as project; it is merely a part. By "fundamental project," one must understand the unity of one's life as projecting oneself toward a future. Every little project is an expression of this fundamental project. Every desire, every act, and each single tendency of the subject reveals the whole person. Using existential psychoanalysis, Sartre thinks that we may compare "the various empirical drives of a subject [in order to] try to discover and disengage the fundamental project which is common to them all – and not by a simple summation or recon-struction of these tendencies; each drive or tendency is the entire person" (BN 721).

AN EXISTENTIAL PSYCHOANALYSIS: *THE FAMILY IDIOT*

Sartre's interest in French novelist Gustave Flaubert (1821–80) dated from his discovery of the novel *Madame Bovary* (1857) in his youth. In Sartre's lengthy study (three volumes published in 1971 and 1972), he explores the question "What can we know of a man today?" Examining the case of Flaubert, he weaves the threads of the fundamental project of becoming a writer. Flaubert enacted this project through every aspect of his life, every action and every choice. Interestingly, the essay was written and published after Sartre revised his view of freedom (see the last section of this chapter). In this study, he considers that, when conducting an existential psychoanalysis, one must try to uncover the fundamental project *in view of* how the situation has shaped the individual. Thus, he is also in search of the sociohistorical factors that shaped Flaubert and led him to make himself as this particular project of being a writer.

The for-itself's being is a nihilation of being. Freedom is the nihilation of the world, of the in-itself. To be free is to be-free-to-act and to be-free-in-the-world. So the project is the expression of the relationship between freedom and world. It is freedom working on the world (creating it) to realize its own project. In this creative act, the human justifies his existence. The project, however, is inherently absurd and gratuitous: there is no pre-existing justification for any act or being. Thus projects are contingently chosen by individuals who find themselves in a world—contingently but *freely*. Being the free contingent choice of an individual who is contingent himself, the project is gratuitous, unwarranted by the situation. It is a free project, but the human consciousness wills it and thus justifies it by this reflective act. That said, however, I could not justify committing a crime, for example, by claiming that it was consistent with my project. I am still always responsible for the actions committed in view of this gratuitous project of mine. This simultaneous gratuitousness and justification of the project is what Sartre calls the "existential vertigo." But it is also authentic existence! Sartre requires that we opt for being free, that we do not flee our freedom in bad faith.

When explaining the notion of vertigo, Sartre associates it with the realization on the part of the individual that one is absolutely free.

This entails that "any conduct on my part is only possible, and this means that while constituting a totality of motives for pushing away that situation, I at the same moment apprehend these motives as not sufficiently effective" (BN 68). The example he gives is of the walker on a narrow path without a guard rail, which goes along a precipice (BN 66). In anguish, and experiencing the vertigo, the walker realizes that although the precipice appears dangerous and should command prudence on his part, it is entirely and equally possible that he be prudent or not. Further, what generates anguish is the realization that he could suddenly decide to throw himself off the cliff—that nothing would prevent that from happening except his own will. He is not determined in his conduct.

Thus, it is somewhat misleading to say that a human being uses his freedom in order to transcend his situation: rather, a human being *is* freedom. Consciousness is absolutely free; consciousness is freedom; consciousness is nothingness. It is freedom and, as such, it is nihilation. It is not bound by anything, but rather it creates the world freely as this intentional free consciousness that encounters the in-itself (as we have discussed it in previous chapters). Sartre goes so far as to say that a prisoner or a person undergoing torture remains free. He said, somewhat provokingly, "We have never been as free as under the German occupation" [my translation of "Jamais nous n'avons été plus libres que sous l'occupation allemande" ["La République du silence," *Situations III*, 11]) To summarize, then, absolute freedom is an ontological fact. That is, I am necessarily and always free by virtue of the fact that I exist as a free consciousness. Practical freedom, however, is to be gained. It is not because one is ontologically free that one will make oneself practically free. One may flee one's freedom and freely choose to be in bad faith, as we will see in Chapter 4.

THE FREEDOM OF JOE CHRISTMAS

In *Being and Nothingness*, Sartre quotes a passage from American writer William Faulkner's *Light in August* (1932) in which Joe Christmas, a black man, has been beaten up and castrated by a group of people. He lies on the floor, injured and dying, and looks at his torturers: "For a long moment he looked up at them with peaceful and unfathomable and unbearable eyes" (cited in BN 526). Sartre quotes this in the context of his discussion of concrete relations between individuals, specifically sadism. He explains the sadist's project as one of subduing the freedom of the Other (something we will see further in Chapter 5). He says: "Thus this explosion of the Other's look in the world of the sadist causes the meaning and goal of sadism to collapse. The sadist discovers that it was that freedom which he wished to enslave, and at the same time he realizes the futility of his efforts" (BN 526–7). One's freedom cannot be attained by the acts of an Other. One remains free even under torture. Obviously Christmas is not free to act, i.e., to stand up and leave. But he remains a free consciousness that can look onto the Other and give meaning to his world.

FREEDOM AND RESPONSIBILITY

Ontological freedom, as described in *Being and Nothingness*, extends into an ethical, practical freedom to which responsibility is tied. Because freedom is conceived of as absolute, yet also in the practical realm of action, Sartre calls it a condemnation: "We are condemned to be free." He explains this formula in the following: "Condemned, because he did not create himself, yet, in other respects is free; because, once thrown into the world, he is responsible for everything he does" (EH 23). For him, freedom is not something that we can escape. It is a fundamental structure of the for-itself: we are as free. If I am absolutely free, however, I am also entirely responsible; I am not determined by anything; there is no transcendent order determining me. We have seen in the previous chapter that Sartre embraces atheism. As a result, I am not determined by a God. Similarly, I am also free from determination by society or my situation in the world. I can do what I want with it, in the sense that I can give it the meaning I want. Therefore, my being born in a destitute family of alcoholic parents in a neighborhood that claims high crime rates does not preclude me from becoming a successful person with college degrees in my pocket. Nor does a cozy financial situation determine me to become a successful businessperson. I can make myself regardless of my situation: my situation is mine. I have chosen it and it is as a freedom that I have done so. To Sartre, there are no non-human situations. He writes:

> The situation is *mine* because it is the image of my free choice of myself, and everything which it presents to me is *mine* in that this represents me and symbolizes me. Is it not I who decide the coefficient of adversity in things and even their unpredictability by deciding myself?
>
> Thus there are no *accidents* in a life; a community event which suddenly bursts forth and involves me in it does not come from the outside. If I am mobilized in a war, this war is *my war*; it is in my image and I deserve it. I deserve it first because I could always get out of it by suicide or by desertion; these ultimate possibles are those which must always be present for us when there is a question of envisaging a situation. For lack of getting out of it, I have *chosen* it.
>
> (BN 708)

This passage emphasizes well the view of freedom as fundamental and absolute. Further, because of this absolute freedom, I am to be held responsible for my situation (it is "I" who made it), for my choices (they are not imposed on me since I am not determined), and for what I do with myself, since "Man is nothing else but what he makes of himself" (EH 15). According to Sartre, I cannot, no matter how much I would prefer, blame my situation or any other factor to excuse my way of being. He offers a clear and concise argument supporting this in his public lecture *Existentialism is a Humanism*. He explains that a coward is such only because he has made himself a coward: "There's no such thing as a cowardly constitution" (EH 34). People would like to be able to appeal to such excuses because the thought that one has to be responsible for everything is frightening. But Sartre insists:

> What the existentialist says is that the coward makes himself cowardly, that the hero makes himself heroic. There's always a possibility for the coward not to be cowardly any more and for the hero to stop being heroic. What counts is total involvement; some one particular action or set of circumstances is not total involvement.
>
> (EH 35)

GARCIN'S COWARDICE

In the play *No Exit* (1944), three characters arrive after their deaths as prisoners of a room in the afterworld. It appears that they have the capacity of spying on what happens on Earth. Garcin listens to a conversation about him among his friends on Earth and is unhappy to find out that they now think of him as a coward. He complains that they make this judgment on the basis of one act (presumably his last). Inès, another character in the play, provokes him and he says: "I died too soon. I wasn't allowed time to do my deeds." To which she replies: "One always dies too soon—or too late. And yet one's whole life is complete at that moment, with a line drawn neatly under it, ready for the summing up. You are—your life, and nothing else" (*No Exit* 43). Garcin may have dreamed of himself as a hero, but what matters are his deeds and they make him into a coward. He must bear the responsibility for his cowardice because his deeds are the outcome of his free choices.

We make ourselves, there is no predetermined essence of the human being, the for-itself constantly thrusts himself forward and never is what it is. It is always in the making. It is an existence that exists and becomes an essence only at the moment of death (this is the meaning of the phrase "existence precedes essence").

"EXISTENCE PRECEDES ESSENCE"

This Sartrean phrase is often used to define existentialism, and by Sartre himself too. As we have seen in the previous chapter, Sartre defines the for-itself, in *Being and Nothingness*, as a being that is not what it is and is what it is not. The for-itself is a project, it is in the making, it makes itself. Therefore, it exists before being anything. One can define a human being only provisionally as this human being lives. For, there is always a chance that this person will change radically. However, once life is over, once one ceases to exist, one can be defined, and this definition will be true forever. One will have an essence. For example, one could claim that the essence of my being is to be a philosophy professor who writes books. However, because I am alive I may radically change my orientation and become a baker. It is only once I am dead and we can sum up my deeds that we can say what I was.

Man must acknowledge this freedom. If he does, he will be authentic—but he will also be anguished. This anguish is sometimes too much to bear, and this is why we will attempt to flee from it as Sartre explains. We are often tempted to find excuses, to think of ourselves as being determined. When we do, we are in bad faith. We will return to all this in more detail in Chapter 4.

Sartre has explored the problem posed by freedom and responsibility, and the anguish it generates, quite beautifully in his novels and plays. Two plays in particular illustrate the inner workings of absolute freedom as it is presented in *Being and Nothingness*: *The Flies* (1943) and *The Devil and the Good Lord* (1951). In the first, the emphasis is placed on the tie between freedom and responsibility; the second explores the consequences of atheism, one of which being the liberation of human beings.

BEAUVOIR ON ABSOLUTE FREEDOM

Simone de Beauvoir and Sartre had numerous discussions while Sartre was elaborating his ideas to be included in *Being and Nothingness*. Notably, Beauvoir recounts the discussion they had in the early part of 1940, regarding the notion of absolute freedom. Sartre was on leave from the army and they met in Paris. They had a heated exchange in which Sartre was defending the view that consciousness is always absolutely free, a view that eliminates any weight of the situation. Beauvoir says:

> During the days that followed we discussed certain specific problems, in particular the relationship between "situation" and freedom. I maintained that from the angle of freedom as Sartre defined it—that is, an active transcendence of some given context rather than mere stoic resignation—not every situation was equally valid: what sort of transcendence could a woman shut up in a harem achieve? Sartre replied that even such a cloistered existence could be lived in several quite different ways. I stuck to my point for a long time, and in the end made only a token submission. Basically I was right. But to defend my attitude I should have had to abandon the plane of individual, and therefore idealistic, morality on which we had set ourselves.
>
> (*Prime of Life* 434)

In her writings on ethics, *Pyrrhus and Cinéas* and *The Ethics of Ambiguity* as well as in her *magnum opus The Second Sex*, Beauvoir shows

THE FREE ORESTES AND GOETZ

In *The Flies*, the main character claims to be free. He does not recognize any powers from the gods and even if the transcendent realm still exists for him it is completely ineffective. He acknowledges that Jupiter has created him, but at the same time says: "But you blundered; you should not have made me free." Jupiter answers that freedom was granted to man only so that he could serve his god; Orestes replies: "Perhaps. But now it has turned against its giver. […] Neither slave nor master. I *am* my freedom. No sooner had you created me than I ceased to be yours" (*Flies* 117). Orestes is freed from divine oppression. He is absolutely free, and lays claim to his deeds. He agrees with himself, taking full responsibility for his actions, and does not suffer from any guilt, unlike his sister Electra or the good people of Argos who are persecuted by the flies. Orestes explains that once he had discovered that he was free, there was nothing "left in Heaven, no right or wrong, nor anyone to give me orders" (*Flies* 118). He had no other choice but to follow his own path and create his own values by making choices. Orestes is the embodiment of the ontological absolute freedom as defined in *Being and Nothingness*. Further, he is an authentic man since he does not attempt to deny his freedom and assumes full responsibility for his choices and deeds.

Another major character in Sartre's theater attempts to be authentic in this way and we have been introduced to him briefly in the preceding chapter. Goetz in *The Devil and the Good Lord* undergoes an interesting evolution. At the beginning of the play, he does evil in order to oppose God, which means he is not authentically evil since he needs an opposite. The character of Catherine asks him why he chooses evil and his answer is, because the good has already been done! God does the good and Goetz, being a creator, does evil. But he does not really invent as he positions himself against God. He defies the power of God. But once he is challenged himself to do good deeds, he embraces bad faith and forces himself to follow the commands of a transcendent morality: he tries to accomplish good, but this good is not of his own making. Goetz struggles for a while until he discovers that "Heaven is an empty hole" (Devil 112). He exclaims: "God doesn't exist [...] I have delievered us. No more Heaven, no more Hell; nothing but earth" (Devil 141–2). Goetz has discovered that man is alone and abandoned and that he must decide, on his own, about good and evil. Sartre emphasizes the link between atheism and freedom in this play, something he had argued for in *Existentialism is a Humanism*. The message of his play is that one is always alone, and that to believe that God is there to decide about good and evil is to fool oneself. The individual must take full responsibility and be free in a world that is fundamentally amoral and strictly human. In an interview, Sartre described Goetz's moral becoming in the following: "The path that Goetz follows is that of freedom: it leads from the belief in God to atheism, from an abstract morality [...] to concrete commitment" [My translation of "Le chemin que suit Goetz est un chemin de la liberté: il mène de la croyance en Dieu à l'athéisme, d'une morale abstraite [...] à un engagement concret." (Sartre, Jean-Paul, *Un théâtre de situations*, Paris, Gallimard, 1973, p. 315]. This path frees the individual and leads him to actualize his freedom. This path ends "beyond good and evil." By living and assuming atheism, Goetz takes on the role of a freedom that creates values. Interestingly, however, Sartre had already expressed some doubts about the possibility of absolute freedom in the practical realm by the time he wrote that play. Although he still thinks that, ontologically, freedom is absolute, he begins to change his mind regarding moral freedom and accounts more and more for the role of situation. This begins in the late forties and is expressed more fully in his later writings. We can see seeds of this change in the three novels that form *The Roads to Freedom*.

FRIEDRICH NIETZSCHE'S *BEYOND GOOD AND EVIL* (1886)

The German philosopher Friedrich Nietzsche was a staunch atheist. His 1886 essay *Beyond Good and Evil* proposes that human beings adopt a new moral stance that is no longer simply adopting the categories "good" and "evil" as defined by Christian morality. Nietzsche's philosopher of the future and ideal human being, the *Übermensch*, will create his own values as a free being. This moral person will freely invent his own morality, which will be the source of all values. This kind of morality is deemed to be "beyond good and evil" as it abandons these categories for the individual to flourish as a free and authentic being. The individual is no longer under the yoke of a transcendent morality dictated by a God who is now declared to be dead. Nietzsche explores further the origins and meaning of the notions of good and evil, and good and bad, in his *Genealogy of Morals* (1887).

THE FAILURE OF ABSOLUTE FREEDOM? THE CASE OF MATHIEU

The trilogy *The Roads to Freedom* (which would be better translated as "The Roads *of* Freedom") deals with many characters' existential anxieties. Mathieu Delarue, the main protagonist, dreams of actualizing himself as an absolutely free being. He tries to escape the weight of situations but, in so doing, he confuses genuine freedom with absolute license. He acts whimsically, and believes these acts to be genuine free deeds. He fails to take responsibility for many of his deeds, and is thus shown to be in bad faith. Mathieu undergoes major changes from his early individualistic position, which seeks to actualize absolute freedom. In the third part of the trilogy, *Iron in the Soul*, Mathieu comes to realize that he has been free for nothing. The absolute freedom that he has exercised was in vain. His numerous acts were not true deeds because he was detached, he was not committed. One is committed when one engages oneself fully in one's act and understands that act to have a fundamental bearing on one's existence: one understands that each act contributes to making oneself what one is. Freedom is in vain if it is not committed. Mathieu exclaims that a whimsical act, or a "rash impulse ... that wasn't liberty" (Iron 178). He realizes this after reflecting on his past actions, on what he considered to be meaningful and important. But his past deeds were all non-committed deeds, hence not deeds at all. Thereafter, he decides to commit himself via military combat. Mathieu becomes a French soldier at war against Germany in World War II. However, as he realizes, his forthcoming death is a death for nothing. He rationalizes his decision, saying that he wants his death to mean that it is impossible to live. However, this is only a transitory stage for Mathieu. The decisive transformation is yet to occur in the episode of the bell-tower. Mathieu is stuck with other soldiers in the bell-tower of a village. Germans are coming through the village and their little group attacks them. During this episode, Mathieu shoots a German soldier and kills him. This deed, as he says, is a trace of his life. The dead man is *his* "work." At this moment, Mathieu has finally fully integrated his own situatedness. Being a soldier at war, he commits the deed of a soldier at war: he kills an enemy. He then fully embodies the violence of history, the violence of his situation as a being caught in the historical whirlwind of war. At this moment, he becomes a situated freedom; he is fully committed. He also assumes full responsibility for his action: the corpse is "his" doing. The episode concludes with this statement: "He fired.[...] He was all-powerful. He was free" (Iron 225). The bell-tower is destroyed by bombing. This is how the episode ends. The reader is left thinking that Mathieu died in the bell-tower. Drafts of a fourth volume of *The Roads to Freedom* reveal that Mathieu was only injured. But the general reader of the novels does not know this and there is no indication in the remainder of the third volume that Mathieu had survived the attack—so the reader is left thinking that he died. This death is meaningful in many ways. One of the most interesting ways of interpreting the death of Mathieu, the existentialist "hero," is as the failure of individualism and absolute freedom. One cannot make oneself absolutely free regardless of one's situatedness and regardless of others—something that Mathieu has attempted throughout the novels.

EVOLUTION OF THE NOTION OF FREEDOM

In an interview for the *New Left Review* in 1969, Sartre expressed his surprise at the rigidity of his moral demands as they were expressed in the philosophy and in the novels and the plays of the forties. About these plays, which he identifies with the label "theatre of freedom," he says:

> The other day, I re-read a prefatory note of mine to a collection of these plays—*Les Mouches*, *Huis Clos* and others—and was truly scandalized. I had written: "Whatever the circumstances, and wherever the site, a man is always

free to choose to be a traitor or not … " When I read this, I said to myself: it's incredible, I actually believed that!

(Itinerary 4–5)

Sartre's astonishment toward himself is to be explained by the transformation that his view of freedom underwent. Sartre evolved from a notion of absolute freedom to one that truly takes into account the weight of situation. This shift in his views is due to a number of factors. One of them is Sartre's personal discovery of his own historicity when he participated in the war. True enough, this occurred in 1939 and 1940; one would have expected to see a less stringent notion of freedom in the treatise published in 1943. But as Sartre matures and becomes more and more politically committed, and as he explores the possibility of authenticity and free action in his plays, such as *Dirty Hands* and *Unburied Dead*, he gradually abandons it. His struggle with the notion of authenticity in his *Notebooks for an Ethics* may also have played a role, as he came to realize that a morality of absolute freedom might be impossible (something we will examine in the following chapters). His theoretical flirtation with Marxism and his re-thinking of the for-itself's relations with others in the *Critique of Dialectical Reason* (1960) were also crucial. These transformations led him to say, in 1969, in the same interview quoted above:

The idea which I have never ceased to develop is that in the end one is always responsible for what is made of one. Even if one can do nothing else besides assume this responsibility. For I believe that a man can always make something out of what is made of him. This is the limit I would today accord to freedom: the small movement which makes of a totally conditioned social being someone who does not render back completely what his conditioning has given him.

(Itinerary 7)

This is a significant change from the view expressed in *Being and Nothingness* in 1943.

SUMMARY

Sartre proposed a powerful view of the human being as absolutely free. We have seen that this freedom entails absolute responsibility as a correlate. His view, as originally expounded in *Being and Nothingness*, was problematic in that it left little room for the weight of the situation. Indeed, Sartre argued that freedom is always situated while at the same time insisting on freedom as absolute and largely unaffected by its situation. This is because he wanted to make the case for the absence of determinism. The only determinism there can be is that of the individual's choice of interpreting his situation one way rather than another. In later writings, Sartre acknowledged the importance of situation in shaping individuals to a certain extent. He revised his definition of freedom to say that freedom is what allows us to make something out of what we have been made to be. Whether absolute or situated, freedom must be embraced by the individual. The absolute responsibility that this entails, however, triggers anguish. The individual may be tempted to escape this anguish by embracing bad faith, i.e. by not recognizing himself as free. This, however, is not acceptable for Sartre, who thinks individuals should strive to be authentic, the subject of the next chapter.

4

AUTHENTICITY

In the previous chapters, we have seen that Sartre defines the human being as an intentional consciousness that is absolutely free. Consciousness is in the world and acts freely, surpassing its facticity toward a being that it is not. Consciousness is what it is not and is not what it is. It aims toward a future possible and is thus also defined as being a project that transcends itself. Because consciousness is absolutely free, it can transcend its own situation, its facticity, and become what it chooses to be through its actions. As we have seen, however, absolute freedom entails absolute responsibility. The lack of a transcendent being such as God condemns the human being to act by himself and create values for himself; but this makes him entirely responsible for his deeds. Because the human being is the sum of his deeds, the human being is thus entirely responsible for what he makes of himself.

Sartre is fully aware that the individual who is aware of this might be crushed by the weight of his absolute responsibility. He acknowledges that, most of the time, individuals will have recourse to bad faith to hide their own freedom from themselves. The responsibility that follows from our absolute freedom is tremendous, and it is always tempting to try to escape it by making use of self-deception. Bad faith can be understood in two different ways. First, ontologically, bad faith is said to be an unavoidable state for the for-itself. Second, ethically, bad faith is presented as something the for-itself ought to avoid while striving for authenticity. Authenticity is the key to Sartrean—and most existentialist—ethics. If bad faith is a permanent state of being for the for-itself, however, authenticity might be impossible to achieve. We are facing a major problem.

In this chapter, we will first examine the meanings of bad faith. In this context, the famous Sartrean example of the café waiter will be analyzed. We will then consider the ethical aspect of bad faith and contrast it with authenticity. We will look at an early Sartrean critique of inauthenticity in *Nausea* as he introduces the notion of *salauds* (literally, swine or bastards), and then we will explore the possibility of authenticity by looking at the *Notebooks for an Ethics* and Sartre's discussion of it. Further, we will consider the text *Anti-Semite and Jew*. This chapter concludes with an examination of the possibility of authenticity, and how it forms the ground for an existentialist ethics.

I AM ANGUISHED, THEREFORE I AM?

The concept of bad faith emerges rather early in *Being and Nothingness*. It immediately follows Sartre's definition of consciousness as nothingness and as freedom. Being free, consciousness is anguished. The individual realizes that he is responsible for all his choices and actions, that he is not determined in any way. This responsibility is a heavy weight to bear. As Sartre puts it: "Anguish is precisely my consciousness of being my own future, in the mode of not-being" (BN 68). It is the separation between the for-itself as it "is" now and as it will be, between me and my self (as an essence). As a for-itself, consciousness is what it is not, and is not what it is; it is always at a distance from itself. We have discussed this in earlier chapters. This generates anguish because it opens up possibilities for me, but these possibilities are merely that: possible. These possibilities will be actualized only if I freely make them happen. Sartre writes of two types of anguish: anguish before the future and anguish before the past.

Anguish in the face of the future is experienced when the for-itself realizes that nothing binds him to any course of action. Faced with the possibility to jump off a precipice, "if nothing compels me to save my life, nothing prevents me from precipitating myself into the abyss" (BN 69). The decision will shape my self. I would like to be the self that would bind me to a course of action, but I am not this self just yet; I am not bound to anything; I am free. Anguish is also experienced before the past. Sartre explains it with the example of the gambler. The gambler, whom we have encountered in Chapter 2, has made a firm decision to stop gambling. Yet, the next day, he finds himself near a gaming table. What will he do? At this moment, the gambler appeals to his past resolution to not play in order to guide his decision, but he quickly realizes that the resolution of the previous day is not binding in any way. He has to reiterate his decision not to play at this moment, when confronted with the possibility to play again. The gambler experiences anguish, realizing that he is absolutely free—free to play or not play. Neither my past being, nor a future being, can come to the rescue. In this moment, in this situation, I am free to act—whatever I choose, I am entirely responsible for my choice. Sartre says: "We are always ready to take refuge in a belief in determinism if this freedom weighs upon us or if we need an excuse. Thus we flee from anguish by attempting to apprehend ourselves from without as an Other or as a *thing*" (BN 82). This attempt is bound to fail, however, because we are not to be defined as if we were an Other or a thing. I am in the mode of being what I am not, and so, Sartre says: "It is certain that we can not overcome anguish, for we *are* anguish" (ibid.). We will discuss this notion more in Chapter 6.

BAD FAITH

Given that the human being is fundamentally anguished, and that anguish is a state that any individual would rather escape, it is natural that any individual will attempt to flee anguish. This is what bad faith is, to Sartre: the attempt by consciousness to lie to itself. Therefore, if anguish is the immediate given of my freedom then I cannot eliminate it for, as I am attempting to veil it, I must be paying attention to it. To hide from myself the kind of being I am, I must know what that being is, thus paying attention to it, being aware of it. So to flee anguish, one must be conscious of it in a certain way.

We have said that bad faith is the attempt to lie to oneself about one's freedom. Bad faith is different from lying, however, in that, in bad faith, the distinction between "liar" and "lied to" vanishes: I am the one lying to myself and yet, I believe in the lie. To me, the lie is the truth. When I lie to an Other, however, I know the truth but the lie is projected outside of myself toward an Other. I intend to deceive an Other. Bad faith is different; it is the attempt to deceive *oneself* about what one knows to be true. Sartre calls this state a precarious one. Indeed, for in bad faith, I am also conscious of the lie: fundamentally, I know that the truth I believe in is a lie that I made up for myself. How can one explain that consciousness will lie to itself successfully?

PSYCHOANALYSIS AND BAD FAITH

Psychoanalysis attempts to solve the problem of bad faith by replacing the distinction between "liar" and "lied to" with that of the unconscious "id" and the "ego." Sartre is dissatisfied by this attempt. As we have seen in Chapter 1, he rejects the unconscious. There is simply no room in Sartre's translucid consciousness for such an obscure, inaccessible part. In the psychoanalytic scheme of things, he says, I become an Other to myself. The id is foreign to the ego. By placing bad faith in the realm of the unconscious, psychoanalysis is missing the point, for bad faith happens in consciousness; bad faith is such a problematic attitude to explain because it is a conscious process.

In his analysis of bad faith, Sartre discusses two famous examples. First, he presents us with a romantic rendezvous. A woman has agreed to go out with a man for the first time. Certainly the man has something in mind, and the woman knows this, yet the woman wants to remain oblivious to the man's intentions, as she wants to postpone the moment at which she will have to make a decision. She wants to be admired in her free being, and does not want to acknowledge that she is the object of some sexual desire. The man grabs her hand. What does she do? Withdrawing her hand means saying no to the man; leaving it there means a yes. Both involve a decision she is not ready to make.

> The young woman leaves her hand there, but she *does not notice* that she is leaving it. She does not notice because it happens by chance that she is at this moment all intellect. She draws her companion up to the most lofty regions of sentimental speculation; she speaks of Life, of her life, she shows herself in her essential aspect—a personality, a consciousness. And during this time the divorce of the body from the soul is accomplished; the hand rests inert between the warm hands of her companion—neither consenting nor resisting—a thing.
>
> (BN 97)

She makes of herself a disembodied mind and thus denies her own facticity, her embodied being. She is in bad faith. It serves her well not to acknowledge her being of flesh in this moment if she wishes to postpone the moment of the decision. On other occasions—or maybe later as they are ready to depart—she may freely decide to give in to the man's solicitation, thus fully acknowledging herself and her situation, letting herself experience the pleasures of being desired both as a free and sexed individual, as a mind and a body. But, at this moment, while letting her hand be held by that of the man, she is lying to herself: she *is* body and mind, and yet she plays at being a disembodied mind only.

Another fascinating example that Sartre provides to illustrate the attitude of bad faith is that of the waiter in the café. This is undoubtedly his most famous example.

> Let us consider this waiter in the café. His movement is quick and forward, a little too precise, a little too rapid. He comes toward the patrons with a step a little too quick. He bends forward a little too eagerly; his voice, his eyes express an interest a little too solicitous for the order of the customer. Finally there he returns, trying to imitate in his walk the inflexible stiffness of some kind of automaton while carrying his tray with the recklessness of a tight-rope-walker by putting it in a perpetually unstable, perpetually broken equilibrium which he perpetually re-establishes by a light movement of the arm and hand. All his behavior seems to us a game.
>
> (BN 101)

This example shows us a man who "is playing, he is amusing himself [...] he is playing at *being* a waiter in a café" (BN 102). Indeed, since he is not a waiter in essence (in fact, as a for-itself, he has no essence) he has to make himself such. However, he never *is* a waiter in-itself: that is impossible. As a human being who is fundamentally free, who is not what he is and is what he is not, he could decide all of a sudden to quit the café and become something else other than a waiter. But no, our man conscientiously makes himself into a waiter. All of his gestures are carefully executed so that he can *be* a café waiter. But no matter how hard he tries, he will never be such in the mode of the in-itself. He can never be, he can only exist as a being that becomes what he makes himself to be. He can make it his project to be a waiter, a very good one at that, but he cannot say that he *is* one. He is not his behavior nor is he his conduct. For, as Sartre says, "If I am one [café waiter], this can not be in the mode of being in-itself. I am a waiter in the mode of *being what I am not*" (BN 103). The waiter is playing at *being* a café waiter. Concentrating on the gestures and attitudes, he is dwelling in bad faith; his focus is misplaced. Sartre tells us that the same happens to the student who wants to be attentive. He so "exhausts himself in playing the attentive role that he ends up by no longer hearing anything"(ibid.). The play has taken over.

What Sartre wants to get at here is that when I say that I *am*, I am missing my own being as one that constantly makes itself. To put it differently, by claiming to have a static being (I am), I am denying that I am a dynamic being (I become) who makes itself via its actions. Sartre says that, for consciousness, making sustains being. Hence, consciousness is as making itself: "Consciousness is not what it is" (BN 105).

Is bad faith inevitable? Sartre questions the possibility of sincerity and presents it as yet another instance of bad faith: one plays at being sincere! In both instances—bad faith and sincerity—one is aiming at being in-itself, hence one is fleeing from one's own being. He concludes this section of *Being and Nothingness* on a rather gloomy note, which casts something of a bad spell on his later attempts at delineating an ethics: he says that the being of the human being is one of bad faith. However, in a footnote, Sartre says that authenticity is a human possibility, but he does not explain here how one can achieve it! For that, one must look at his subsequent writings.

LES SALAUDS

In *Nausea*, we find an early formulation of Sartre's views on inauthenticity, or bad faith. The main character, Antoine Roquentin, whom we met earlier in Chapters 1 and 2, is highly critical of the bourgeois of Bouville. On a Sunday morning he goes to see a special show. "A clock strikes half-past ten and I start on my way: Sundays at this hour, you can see a fine show in Bouville, but you must not come too late after High Mass" (N 41). The show is that of the bourgeois families on their Sunday morning walk. All individuals are conscientiously playing their roles in what looks like a choreographed ritual of meetings and greetings. Roquentin walks with the crowd and observes these behaviors. He is not, at this point, very critical, but he has a sharp sense of observation. The ballet that he describes resembles that of the café waiter who, as we have seen, also performs a well-studied choreography while playing at being a café waiter. The bourgeois of Bouville on their Sunday morning walk are also playing at being bourgeois. They are following conventions, they are putting on a mask, and they try to convince themselves that they *are* bourgeois.

The same can be said of the bourgeois whose portraits are hung in one gallery of the Bouville museum. Roquentin visits the museum one day and admires these paintings. The gallery contains the portraits of the notables of the city, the leaders who have made Bouville the flourishing town it is. Roquentin contrasts his own experience of feeling contingent, of being *de trop*, with what seems to be their quiet confidence that they have a right to exist. He says:

> "Then I realized what separated us: [...] I hadn't the right to exist. I had appeared by chance, I existed like a stone, a plant or a microbe. My life put out feelers towards small pleasures in every direction. [...] But for this handsome, faultless man, now dead, for Jean Pacôme, son of the Pacôme of the Défence Nationale, it had been an entirely different matter: the beating of his heart and the mute rumblings of his organs, in his case, assumed the form of rights to be instantly obeyed. For sixty years, without a halt, he had used his right to live. The slightest doubt had never crossed those magnificent grey eyes. Pacôme had never made a mistake."

(N 84)

LUCIEN THE LEADER

Sartre explores the notion of inauthenticity again in his short story "The Childhood of a Leader," one of the stories collected in *The Wall* (1939). Lucien, the main character, evolves through various life-stages to adulthood. He is uncertain about the meaning of his existence, and perplexed by the bourgeois hypocrisy he notices around him. His father is a leader, a factory boss, and he reassures his son that he too will be a leader. There is an "essence" of Lucien as leader, and his whole life sees him moving in this direction. The story illustrates how Lucien comes to realize that he has rights and that he is indeed a leader. The processes of introspection that he underwent as a youth were only misleading. He reflects: "'First maxim,' Lucien said, 'not to try and see inside yourself; there is no mistake more dangerous.'" ("Childhood of a Leader" 142). He now looks for the "real Lucien" in the other's view of him. He thus adopts an objectified view of himself as a leader with rights: "[...] rights were beyond existence, like mathematical objects and religious dogma. And now Lucien was just that: an enormous bouquet of responsibilities and rights" ("Childhood of a Leader" 143). Lucien is also a *salaud* because he is inauthentic.

Convinced of their right to live and that many things are owed them, comfort, monetary security, authority over men, etc., the bourgeois perform their duties and leadership unquestioningly. They conform to an essence of being bourgeois and believe they participate in that essence: they *are* bourgeois and, accordingly, they *have* rights and duties. This is, for them, a natural order of things. They would not think of questioning it—they simply live their existence according to it. Roquentin daydreams about the various figures he sees in the gallery of portraits and, when he has gone through the gallery, he exclaims: "Farewell, beautiful lilies, elegant in your painted little sanctuaries, good-bye lovely lilies, our pride and reason for existing, good-bye you *bastards*!" (N 94, my emphasis).

The *salauds* are those who refuse to acknowledge their freedom. As human beings, they are free consciousnesses that create values as they act. However, they deny this and prefer to adhere to a social order that imposes values on them but that grants them rights by the same token. The *salaud* is in bad faith because he refuses to acknowledge himself as a free for-itself. He does not experience anguish because he sees himself bound to an external order. Not being anguished, he fails to be authentic.

AUTHENTICITY

Given that Sartre has defined the human being as a consciousness that is ever attempting to flee this anguish in bad faith, the question arises as to whether it is at all possible, or even desirable, to be authentic. Why be authentic, one will ask, if it will yield existential suffering? Authenticity is a fundamental value in Sartre's ethical thought; it is what we should strive for as human beings.

SARTRE'S OWN QUEST FOR AUTHENTICITY

Sartre wrote a diary, while a soldier, at Simone de Beauvoir's suggestion. In his diary, Sartre wrote philosophical notes, notes about his readings, and anecdotes about his daily life as a soldier in the meteorological unit. One emerging philosophical theme is that of authenticity. Interestingly, it stems from Sartre's own personal struggles to be authentic. Being confronted with war, he realizes that he has to adopt an attitude toward it. Up to his mobilization, he had been a somewhat apolitical anarchist. His reflections on authenticity are also triggered by his personal life and the problematic relationships he had with the Kosakiewicz sisters (Olga and Wanda) since 1935. He recognizes that he is a buffoon:

> For I am social and an actor – here, no doubt, out of boredom and the need to expend an overflow of boisterousness; elsewhere to win hearts; on other occasions simply to reflect a clearcut image in the eyes of other people.
>
> (WD 18)

He desires, however, to be authentic, to be sincere. But:

> If I question myself, it's in order to write down the results of this examination […]
>
> (WD 29)

Would Sartre's longing for authenticity be itself inauthentic? Is he his own example for the "champion of sincerity"? He pursues his reflection in the following notebooks. After having formulated *historicity* and *commitment*, he says that the authenticity available to him then consists in criticizing

> that freedom in the air which I've so patiently given myself, and uphold the principle that it's necessary to become rooted. By this, I don't mean that it's necessary to prize certain things – since I prize a goodly number of things with all my strength. What I mean is that the personality must have a *content*. It must be made of clay, and I'm made of wind.
>
> (WD 293–4)

Sartre's endeavour is thus to become an authentic, free, and committed individual.

Sartre wrote in a total of 15 notebooks throughout his war experience. Six out of 15 notebooks have been published (the nine unpublished ones are either lost or unfound).

The human being is conceived of as a being that makes itself. It is a project and as such, it aims towards a possible being, it aims toward itself as having accomplished a set of deeds or having become a certain kind of person. The individual aims at a possible that it sets for itself. As freedom, consciousness posits for itself certain goals to be attained and acts, or does not act, to achieve them. In *Notebooks for an Ethics*, Sartre explains that the human being is a project that aims toward authenticity. He does not provide a rationale for why one should aim toward authenticity, rather he posits that it is the case that we are. His reasoning is the following: because the individual aims at being a for-itself-in-itself, that is, because the individual seeks a justification for his existence, he aims to take his own freedom (himself) as the foundation of his being. His aim, accordingly, is to acknowledge his own being as free. It takes an act of will, however, for the individual to make his own freedom an essential part of his project. I have to acknowledge that I am free, and that freedom lies at the heart of my being as a being that makes itself— only then can I be said to be authentic. In addition, however, I also have to accept the responsibility that is entailed by my freedom. The striving for authenticity leads to what Sartre names "existential vertigo." As I strive to be authentic, I experience this existential vertigo because:

> [my] project appears to reflection in its absolute gratuity. But since reflection wills it, it is recaptured. Except it is recaptured as absolute and a totality without ceasing to be gratuitous. It is this double simultaneous aspect of the human project, gratuitous at its core and consecrated by a reflective reprise, that makes it into authentic existence.

> (Notebooks 481)

The authentic individual bears a tremendous responsibility as he must create meaning for himself and for the world. Marjorie Grene explains: "In Sartre, [...] genuine existence is conceived of as free, not in facing death so much as in facing the meaningless ground of its own transcendence; that is, the fact that the values by which I live depend not on divine fiat or metaphysical necessity but on myself alone" (Grene 266). However, it seems that authenticity then is simply the acknowledgment of one's way of being. Ontologically, the individual *is* a freedom. As such, he is the one creating meaning and values—but he must acknowledge that he is. This is the requirement of authenticity;

the failure to recognize oneself as such is bad faith. Thomas Anderson explains quite beautifully:

> No human can cause herself or her world to be necessary. No human can create a meaning and justification for the world that would make it exist by right rather than by chance. In a word, no human can be God [although, as we have seen, this is what the for-itself desires]. However, this should pose no insurmountable problem, for after all, human beings are the only source of meaning in Sartre's universe, and a thoroughly human meaning can be given to one's creation. The authentic person recognizes and wills to do precisely this. […] The authentic person gives her life meaning (*sens*) and value by accepting and affirming herself as the free creator of a meaningful world.
>
> (Anderson, *Sartre's Two Ethics* 58)

As we will see in subsequent chapters, Sartre will delineate his existential ethics on the basis of the fundamental ideal of authenticity. The *ought* of his ethics is authenticity. However, a major stumbling block will stand in the way of the ethics of authenticity: the existence of Others. As we will see in the following chapter, it is far from easy to be authentic when the Other is conceived of as preying on one's free being!

ANTI-SEMITE AND JEW

In 1944, Sartre published a short essay in *Les Lettres françaises*, "La République du silence" (literally, "The republic of silence"). In it, he acknowledged, *en passant*, the suffering of Jews. Sartre reports that, following the publication of the essay, many Jews thanked him for the acknowledgment. He exclaimed: "How completely must they have felt themselves abandoned, to think of thanking an author for merely having written the word 'Jew' in an article!" (A-SJ 78). After that, Sartre set out to write the essay *Anti-Semite and Jew*, which was published in 1946. Many have looked at the essay in hope of finding a formulation of the ethics promised at the end of *Being and Nothingness*. If an ethics, per se, cannot be found in the essay, one can at least find an interesting application of some of the principles elaborated in *Being and Nothingness*. For our purposes, the articulation of the notions of inauthenticity and authenticity in relation to the Jew's experience is very interesting.

Sartre puts it very clearly: nothing ever makes an anti-Semite an anti-Semite.

> Anti-Semitism is a free and total choice of oneself, a comprehensive attitude toward Jews and toward men in general, toward history and society; it is at one and the same time a passion and a conception of the world.
>
> (A-SJ 17)

However, this free choice of himself is not a choice of authenticity. The anti-Semite refuses freedom, "Authentic liberty assumes responsibilities, and the liberty of the anti-Semite comes from the fact that he escapes all of his" (A-SJ 32). In fact, the anti-Semite is anguished, as anybody else is—anguished before his own freedom. Sartre explains that in having posited an absolute evil in the person of the Jew and in spending all his energies fighting this evil, the anti-Semite avoids the problem of determining the good: "Each of his outbursts of rage is a pretext to avoid the anguished search for the Good" (A-SJ 45). But, as we have seen, Sartre conceives of the individual as fundamentally free and creative of values. The anti-Semite's attitude is thus inauthentic; the expression of fear is "fear of the human condition" (A-SJ 54).

The anti-Semite is inauthentic. He flees his own freedom and adopts a worldview in which values are fixed and he is merely an instrument. In *Anti-Semite and Jew*, Sartre defines authenticity as "[consisting] in having a true and lucid consciousness of the situation, in assuming the responsibilities and risks that it involves, in accepting it in pride of humiliation, sometimes in horror and hate" (A-SJ 90). The anti-Semite is faced with this ethical requirement. However, Thomas Martin explains that:

> What is characteristic of the anti-Semite's response to his situation is that he precisely does not have "a true and lucid consciousness of the situation," [Sartre's essential condition for authenticity] but rather develops a view of his situation that clouds over the difficulties it harbors. His response is to adopt Manicheism, a simplistic, irresponsible, and extremist worldview that refuses to examine the complexities of his true situation.
>
> (Martin 87)

What of the Jew? Is he more authentic than the anti-Semite? Not necessarily. He too can fall prey to the temptation of adhering to the pre-fabricated image of him, trying to play at not being the Jew that the others think he is. What is authenticity for the Jew? To live to the fullest of his condition as Jew, to make himself a Jew according to what *he* creates as his Jew-ness.

THE JEWISH QUESTION: AN EARLY SARTREAN ANALYSIS OF OPPRESSION

The French title of *Anti-Semite and Jew* literally translates as "Reflections on the Jewish question"—a historically and emotionally charged title if ever there was one, especially given that Europe had only very recently and brutally realized the extent of the Nazi horror when Sartre published the essay. The problem of anti-Semitism was pressing as he was writing the essay. Survivors of Nazi camps were returning to their hometowns and had to face an anti-Semitism that has been exacerbated under the Nazi occupation of France. The problem Sartre addresses is that of French anti-Semitism and the situation of the French Jew. In the conclusion of the essay, he quotes this statement about segregation in the United States by Richard Wright, the black writer: " 'There is no Negro problem in the United States, there is only a White problem.' In the same way, we must say that anti-Semitism is not a Jewish problem; it is *our* problem" (A-SJ 152). The essay is one of the first of many essays, long and short, in which Sartre will explore pressing social and political issues and thus provide theoretical analyses of oppression. We will return to this when we discuss his notion of commitment and his own political engagement in Chapters 7 and 8.

SUMMARY

Bad faith is an ever-present temptation for the individual: embracing it allows one to escape the anguish triggered by acknowledging oneself as absolutely free, and hence responsible. Human beings tend to lie to themselves and pretend that they are determined in their behavior and actions. Sartre believes that most of the time we are in bad faith. Sincerity is also a form of bad faith where one plays at *being* in good faith. Is authenticity possible, then? It is a fundamental value for Sartre, and the ideal of authenticity is one that all individuals should aspire to. Authenticity lies at the core of a Sartrean existential ethics.

5

INTERPERSONAL
RELATIONS

In the last chapters, we have discussed what it means to be a free for-itself striving for authenticity. However, except for a few mentions of the freedom of the Other in Chapter 3, we have only examined the for-itself in isolation so far. This was important in order for us to have a solid grasp of how Sartre conceives of the individual. But the individual is not alone in the world: there are Others. In *Being and Nothingness*, Sartre also introduces the notion of the Other at a late stage, 300 pages into the book. In this important part of the book, he examines the existence of others and how we encounter them in the world—but also how we engage in concrete relations with them—which, for Sartre, will necessarily lead to conflict. In addition to all this, Sartre explains the body. Indeed, he has not introduced the body in the earlier parts of his book devoted to the for-itself. Why? Simply because he thinks that the body emerges out of my encounter with an Other who objectifies me as an object. The facticity of my body, which we discussed in Chapter 2, is revealed to me via the look of the Other.

In this chapter, I will begin by examining the notion of the Other and of my being-for-others. I will discuss the famous view of the alienating look of the Other and its correlate, that "The essence of the relations between consciousnesses ... is conflict" (BN 555). Following this, I will look into Sartre's discussion of concrete relations with others, including his views on sexual relationships and gender difference. I will close the chapter by briefly addressing the possibility of an ethics given the context of alienation and conflict that emerges when considering the existence of Others. This discussion will be carried over to the next chapter, in which we will sum up Sartre's views on the human condition. But first, the discovery of the existence of others.

I AM NOT ALONE: THE OTHER

After having carefully exposed the various aspects of being for-itself, Sartre turns to the question of the existence of other human beings. Their existence is made meaningful for the individual through certain modes of consciousness such as shame and vulgarity. For example, shame is experienced by a for-itself in its consciousness, but it is necessary that the Other exists in order for shame to be possible. If I was alone in the world, I would have no reason to be ashamed of any of my behavior: it is only because the Other exists that I can feel ashamed of doing something. The Other does not have to be physically present at the moment of performing a deed, however. My mere knowledge of the Other's existence and her potential presence suffice to make me experience shame. "I am ashamed of myself *as I appear* to the Other" (BN 302).

It is as an object that I appear to the Other; my encounter with the Other is that of my body with his. When I meet someone, there is first the physical presence of bodies in a certain spatio-temporal frame. I am a consciousness in my body, and I meet a human body. This human body greets me, or not, looks at me, or not; it is a body "inhabited" by a consciousness: the consciousness of the Other. Sartre says that there is an unbridgeable distance between the for-itself and the Other: the body is that through which I meet the Other, but at the same time it is an obstacle as it prevents me from attaining the Other's consciousness. The relationship between me and the Other is one of exteriority. I am an object for the Other and the Other is an object for me. "The Other [...] is presented in a certain sense as the radical negation of my experience, since he is the one for whom I am not subject but object" (BN 310). This object-ness is of a peculiar kind, however: I do not literally become an object for the Other. The Other sees me as an object in his world just as I objectify him in my world, but at the same time, we both know that we are dealing with an object of a different kind than, say, a tree or a desk. Where, then, does the difference lie? Just as I can see the Other, the Other can see me. He is an "object" that looks at me.

THE LOOK

It is in the context of explaining how we are always looked at that
Sartre exposes one of his most famous examples: the voyeur. "Let us
imagine that moved by jealousy, curiosity or vice I have just glued my
ear to the door and looked through a keyhole" (BN 347). The voyeur
who is looking through the keyhole is his deed. At this moment, his
whole world is composed of himself and whatever it is that he sees in
the room on the other side of the door. The whole situation relates to
him, and he is the sole provider of meaning in this situation. Things
have meaning in relation to him: the keyhole is understood as being an
instrument for the voyeur, and the activities in the room are understood as "to be seen" by the peeping Tom.

However, something suddenly disrupts this fragile equilibrium: "[...]
I hear footsteps in the hall. Someone is looking at me! [...] I now
exist as *myself* for my unreflective consciousness. It is this irruption of
the self which has been most often described: I see *myself* because

The Look:

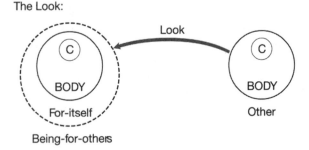

Being-for-others

The Peeping Tom:

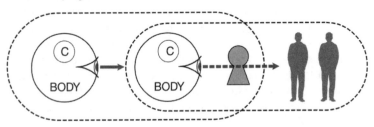

Figure 2

somebody sees me [...]" (BN 349). The presence of the Other disrupts things. I become an object in the world for the Other. If indeed someone is in the hall and is looking at me, I am an object in *his* world. If it is a person who wants to enter the room that I am spying on, I am an obstacle on that person's way. Further, the Other who thus catches me passes judgment on me: "Here is a voyeur." I am objectified and essentialized as being a voyeur. What the Other sees is my body, bent forward, with its eyes looking through a door's keyhole. Where I might have conceived of myself and of my deed as something rightful (I suspect my partner of cheating on me and feel that I am seeking the truth about the matter, for example), the Other's appearance on the scene implies a reinterpretation of my being and my gesture.

Interestingly, Sartre explains that the Other does not have to be physically present. It could be that the "footsteps" I heard were merely the cracking of the wooden floor of an old house. This, however, would only eliminate the "facticity" of the presence of the Other. The experience of feeling looked at unveils that the Other exists for me, whether it be in the corridor and currently watching me or not.

The Other is free to give any meaning to my action that he likes. As a for-itself, the Other is free and sheds meaning on things as he pleases. The look of the Other unto me informs me that I have no control over a part of myself: my being-for-others is strictly determined by others. I am an object among others and have a certain meaning in the Other's world, according to the Other's own project, and there is nothing I can do about it. The presence of the Other makes everything slip; I become an object and my world disintegrates to become his. My possibles, as well as the instruments I use and understand in my situation, are reinterpreted in terms of the Other's situation, they become his situation:

> The ensemble "instrument-possibility" made up of myself confronting the instrument, appears to me as surpassed and organized into a world by the Other. With the Other's look the "situation" escapes me [...] I *am no longer master of the situation.*
>
> (BN 355)

It is as if the Other robs me of the world. But the Other also does more: he affects my being. I am other than myself. When I am by myself and in the center of my world, I am what I am not and I am not what I am. However, when the Other appears, I acquire a being: I *am* someone or other and this someone that I am is not of my own making. This being is my being-for-others. It is:

> My Me-as-object—[it] is not an image cut off from me and growing in a strange consciousness. It is a perfectly real being, *my* being as the condition of my selfness confronting the Other and of the Other's selfness confronting me.
>
> (BN 380)

This being-for-others is not my creation and yet I have to assume responsibility for it, as it obviously is a part of my being. The Other is an alienating figure as it throws me and my world off, by making this being-for-others appear and by making the world his. The initial encounter with the Other thus seems an unpleasant one as I "lose control" over things.

"HELL IS OTHER PEOPLE!"

We have said earlier that the encounter with the Other is that of two bodies. I meet an object in the world and that object is one of flesh that indicates a consciousness. Sartre says that my sense experience allows me to perceive the body of the Other. As unpleasurable as it might be, this encounter still allows me to know more about myself: I first exist as my body (as an embodied consciousness), and then this embodied consciousness meets the Other who, in return, informs me of my body as an object. "The shock of the encounter with the Other is for me a revelation in emptiness of the existence of my body outside as an in-itself for the Other" (BN 461).

Through an analysis of the concrete relations with others, Sartre comes to the harsh conclusion that "The essence of the relations between consciousnesses ... is conflict" (BN 555).

BEAUVOIR'S *SHE CAME TO STAY*

In her first published novel, *She Came to Stay* (1943), Beauvoir explores the problem of interpersonal relationships and, more precisely, the problem of the existence of the Other as a conscious being. Her main character, Françoise, is confronted by the presence of Xavière. Things are complicated in the novel by the fact that Françoise and Xavière are engaged in a love triangle with Françoise's life partner, Pierre. Underlying the feelings of jealousy and competition between the two women is the problem that the other consciousness "holds a secret" about oneself. The epigraph of the novel is from Hegel, and reads: "Each consciousness pursues the death of the Other." The novel ends with the murder of Xavière by Françoise, thus illustrating the conflictual nature of interpersonal relations and fulfilling Hegel's pronouncement. However, this is not illustrative of Beauvoir's own positions as elaborated in her ethical writings following the novel and in her famous *The Second Sex* (1949). In those, she will rather emphasize notions of ambiguous intersubjectivity and the fact that one always needs the Other as a free consciousness in order to flourish as a human being. She thus eventually departs from the Sartrean positions, as we have explained them here.

Because the Other holds a secret about me, knows something of me as an in-itself that I have no access to (I am an object for him), I may adopt one of two attitudes in my relations with him. The first one is an attempt to transcend the Other's transcendence, i.e. to deny the Other's freedom, while the second one is an attempt to incorporate it, i.e. to try to capture the freedom of the Other. Both aim at the dissolution of the Other as such. Thus relations of love, language and masochism (the first attitude), and relations of indifference, desire, hate and sadism (the second attitude), are all attempts by the for-itself to free itself from the alienation caused by the Other. Likewise, Sartre explains, the Other engages in such relations in an attempt to free herself from me. These relations and attitudes are reciprocal, and express the fundamental nature of human relationships as conflictual.

ALL YOU NEED IS LOVE?

In *Being and Nothingness*, in the chapter "Concrete Relations With Others," Sartre explains how we form relations with others, given the initial conflict that he has delineated so well. He says that these relations are ruled by my attitude toward my own being-for-others, i.e. my self as perceived by the Other: the Other sees me; I can try to deny being looked at. If I make the Other into an object, I destroy the look and my own objectivity for the Other. Or else I can try to seize the freedom of the Other, to captivate it, to subjugate it. Sartre says:

> The Other *looks* at me and as such he holds the secret of my being, he knows what I *am*. Thus the profound meaning of my being is outside of me, imprisoned in an absence. [...] in so far as the Other as freedom is the foundation of my being-in-itself, I can seek to recover that freedom and to possess it without removing from it its character as freedom. In fact if I could identify myself with that freedom which is the foundation of my being-in-itself, I should be to myself my own foundation.

(BN 473)

As you will remember, this is exactly the profound desire of the for-itself: to be a for-itself-in-itself (see Chapter 2). The individual thus pursues love in hope to fulfill this fundamental ontological longing.

We will examine one example among the few that Sartre writes about: that of love. Love, one of the most fundamental relations amongst individuals, is, for Sartre, an attempt at assimilating the freedom of the Other. The union with the Other may be impossible because I can never really reach the consciousness of the Other, but I can try my best to put a "spell" on the freedom of the Other, to be as close as possible to a fusion. The fusion is the ideal of love as Sartre puts it, but at the same time, it is an impossible ideal to realize. Love aims at possessing the consciousness of the Other, but the lover aims at the freedom of the Other, the freedom that is his consciousness. Thus, the lover cannot be aiming at possessing the Other as an object; it is the *subjectivity* of the Other that is sought. What is aimed at is a freedom (the freedom of the Other) that would play at being subdued. In doing so, the lover presents himself as a limit to the freedom of the beloved. I want to be the limit that the Other recognizes to his own freedom. What is really interesting, however, is what he explains a little later. By wanting to be loved, the lover wants to gain a feeling of security. I want to be "safe" in the consciousness of the Other. Wanting to be loved is the same as wanting to tame the look of the Other—the consciousness of the Other that puts me in danger by objectifying me and by taking the world away from me. If I am loved, I am no longer an instrument for the Other. The Other encounters my facticity, i.e. my body in situation, and yet, I am more than just an object for him if the Other loves me. Sartre says:

> From this point of view [that of the first attitude], my being must escape the look of the beloved, or rather it must be the object of a look with another structure. I must no longer be seen on the ground of the world as a "this"

The look of the Other no longer petrifies me if I am loved: this is
why we seek to be loved. Love "saves" my facticity and saves me from
alienation. It saves my facticity insofar as the Other has made an
absolute choice of me. The Other thus justifies my presence in the
world. Since Sartre has explained that our presence in the world is
unjustified and completely contingent, what the Other can accomplish
for me seems very important: it might alleviate my anguish.

We thus seek to be loved with good reasons: love saves us from alienation and justifies our existence. How does one gain this redeeming
love of the Other? This is the problem of seduction. Seduction is the
attempt to subjugate the Other's consciousness in making myself into a
fascinating object. I objectify myself and try to capture the Other's
subjectivity via this object of seduction that I create with myself. The
sad thing, though, is that it seems that seduction is bound to fail.
Remember that my being-for-others is something I have no control
over. In objectifying myself to seduce the Other, I have little control
over how the Other will perceive me. It remains his call to determine
the meaning of my expressions. My language as well as my body for
the Other is something I do not know. I may try to manipulate it so
that the Other will be trapped by it, but the final call remains his.

In his discussion of seduction, Sartre concludes that fascination is
not the same as love. One can be fascinated by an object without loving
it. Hence, we need something more than seduction. To love, he says, is to
have the project of being loved. But that entails a problem, as he explains:

The lover is held captive in a wholly different way. He is the captive of his very
demand since love is the demand to be loved; he is a freedom which wills
itself a body and which demands an outside, hence a freedom which imitates
the flight toward the Other, a freedom which qua freedom lays claim to its
alienation. The lover's freedom, in his very effort to make himself be loved as
an object by the Other, is alienated by slipping into the body-for-others; that is,
it is brought into existence with a dimension of flight toward the Other.

(BN 488–9)

The ideal of the love relationship is thus an alienated freedom. In the relationship, each participant wishes to be an object, in order for the other's freedom to alienate itself. One loves and one wants that the Other loves:

> Each one wants the other to love him but does not take into account the fact that to love is to want to be loved and that thus by wanting the other to love him, he only wants the other to want to be loved in turn.

(BN 489)

In this process, we are seeking an impossible fusion of con- sciousnesses. The problem of the Other and of my being-for-other remains unsolved. Further, whatever we gain through the love-rela- tionship is perpetually in danger of being lost. The Other may sud- denly consider me as an object or I may do the same to the Other, in which case the bond is destroyed. Furthermore, a third person may objectify both members of the couple by interrupting the scene and looking at them. Sartre thus concludes that love is a fragile thing and a vain pursuit.

This is very clearly expressed in the play *No Exit*, which we have discussed already in previous chapters. The characters of Garcin, Estelle and Inès are in the afterlife and their situation becomes hell as they find themselves at the mercy of the Other. Locked up in a room for their afterlife, the characters cannot sleep or close their eyes. It is one of the first things that Garcin realizes upon arriving in the room, that he will have to "live" with his eyes wide open. Being in the presence of others, it is impossible to escape the look of the Other. Thus, "each of us will act as torturer of the two others." (No Exit 17). They look at each other and see each other, but, as Sartre has explained, they have little control over their image. Estelle, who is highly dependent on what others think of her, is still anxious before Ines' look: "I'm going to smile, and my smile will sink down into your pupils, and heaven knows what it will become." (No Exit 20–1). As the play unfolds, and discussions and quarrel occur, Garcin and Estelle try to form a coalition against Inès. But this is bound to fail, as Inès reminds them quickly, since, "I'm here, and watching. I shan't take my eyes off you, Garcin; when you're kissing her, you'll feel them boring into you." (No Exit 35). Further in the play she insists that "I'm watching you, [...] I'm a crowd all by myself" (No Exit 45). Garcin, realizing that no alliance is possible, that one will always be looking at the Other, that he will be constantly looked at and thus objectified, exclaims: "There's no need for red-hot pokers. Hell is – other people!" (*No Exit* 45). While one might attempt to explain this by pointing to the trio formed by the characters and the inherent difficulties of such triangular relationships, Sartre thinks that any relations are bound to fail, including the most intimate ones between lovers.

SEXUAL RELATIONS: VIEWS ON GENDER

One would think that the most intimate relations between individuals—love and sexual relations—would have the potential to be positive and non-conflictual. However, Sartre draws a different picture: love and sexual relations are yet other attempts at seducing and capturing the consciousness and freedom of the Other. One uses one's body as an instrument by objectifying itself in an attempt to seduce the Other. I make my own flesh into a fascinating object to captivate the Other, but we have to keep in mind what was said earlier about the unbridgeable distance between consciousnesses. All one can encounter, ultimately, is the body of the Other. Desire aims at the Other's consciousness but this consciousness is embodied; the body of the Other is desirable as an unveiling of her consciousness. This encounter of flesh is the encounter of consciousnesses that are sexed bodies. What does Sartre make of the sexuality of the for-itself? And what does this unveil about his views on sexual difference?

He explains that our sexual attitudes lie at the foundation of all other attitudes, and that sexuality is as fundamental as the upsurge of the for-itself. The human being is sexual from the beginning. To Sartre, then, we exist sexually for each other. Although he acknowledges this, and is ready to define the human being primarily as a sexual being, he does not take the extra step of acknowledging sexual difference. He says that the for-itself is fundamentally sexual, but does not touch on the question of the relationship between sex and gender, or how one's sex must necessarily color the way one exists. If a consciousness is always embodied, the sex of that body is far from indifferent. Sartre discusses desire and explains that while I desire, I unveil "simultaneously *my* being-sexed and *his* being-sexed, *my* body as sex and *his* body" (BN 500). This unveiling of sex remains strangely asexual, however, as Sartre does not explore the implications of sexual difference. Further, the body's sexuality is relegated to the background as he emphasizes the sexuality of consciousness. It is truly as if one's sexuality is fundamental but at the same time indifferent!

When Sartre discusses sexual differences, he does not conduct a philosophical analysis of them; rather he seems to adopt stereotypical views of the sexes. He could have saved himself from stereotyping, since, on one occasion at least, he went beyond the stereotypes by talking about the male sexual organ as passive. The stereotypical view has it that, in intercourse, the female is passive while the male is active. When discussing coitus, however, Sartre refers to a passivity of the penis. To him, it is the whole body, as embodied *consciousness*, that puts the sexual organ in motion. By itself, the sexual organ is passive and cannot act. The penis and vagina are both passive. However, Sartre falls back into sexist, stereotypical views as soon as he talks of the female sexual organs as holes.

To Sartre, holes are "appeals of being." Consciousness perceives them as "having-to-be-filled." He explains that the "natural" tendency of every child is to try to fill holes it encounters by sticking some part of its body in them. The sucking of the thumb becomes, in Sartre's analysis, the attempt of the for-itself to be a fullness of being by plugging the hole that is the mouth:

> The hole is originally presented as a nothingness 'to be filled' with my own flesh; the child can not restrain himself from putting his finger or his whole arm into the hole. It presents itself to me as the empty image of myself.
>
> (BN 781)

Now, for Sartre, the female sexual organ is such a hole and, as such, it is an appeal of flesh, specifically the male flesh, to fill it.

SLIME

The female sexual organ is presented by Sartre as a hole but it is also secreting mucus of a slimy nature. Sartre explains that consciousness's reaction to slime is one of disgust. Because slime is a sort of intermediary state between being in-itself and existence, it represents for consciousness the possibility of being dissolved in the in-itself. While this could be appealing, given our profound desire to be for-itself-in-itself, free consciousness is afraid of the possibility that it faces of being "glued" in the slime. Sartre says that slime is the "revenge of the in-itself," and that the individual that takes the risk of touching it "risk[s] being dissolved in sliminess" (BN 777). For consciousness, the horror of slime is the same as the horror of stagnation: the slimy substance that sticks to oneself stops the individual's upsurge. Consciousness that is a project and that is transcending itself is horrified by the stickiness of the slimy. For the male consciousness, there are thus two reasons to be scared by the female sex: the vagina is a hole that wishes to devour it, and the mucus that it secretes threatens to swallow and stall the movement of transcendence of its consciousness.

The following passage is laden with a chauvinistic and sexist view of sexuality—one that feminist critiques like to target. It presents the vagina as a hole threatening to the male human being:

> The obscenity of the feminine sex is that of everything which "gapes open." It is *an appeal to being* as all holes are. In herself, woman appeals to a strange flesh which is to transform her into a fullness of being by penetration and dissolution. Conversely woman senses her condition as an appeal precisely because she is "in the form of a hole." This is the true origin of Adler's complex. Beyond any doubt her sex is a mouth and a voracious mouth which devours the penis—a fact which can easily lead to the idea of castration. The amorous act is the castration of the man; but this is above all because sex is a hole. We have to do here with a *pre-sexual* contribution which will become one of the components of sexuality as an empirical, complex, human attitude but which far from deriving its origin from the sexed being has nothing in common with basic sexuality, the nature of which we have explained in Part Three. Nevertheless the experience with the hole, when the infant sees the reality, includes the ontological presentiment of sexual experience in general; it is with his flesh that the child stops up the hole and the hole, before all sexual specification, is an obscene expectation, an appeal to the flesh.

> (BN 782)

FEMINIST CRITICISM OF SARTRE

While feminists have been very critical of Sartre, accusing him of misogyny, ideological sexism, and patriarchal existentialism (thanks to the passage on holes and slime in particular) some, like Bonnie Burstow, think that Sartre is merely guilty of "incidental sexism"—which would be understandable to see at work in a man of his time. These feminist critics think that the charge against Sartre is simply overblown. More interestingly, some feminist critics, for example Phyllis Morris and Linda Bell, have reappropriated Sartre's philosophy and used it to rethink the nature of oppression. Indeed, his notions of freedom along with his analysis of oppression and objectification at the hand of the Other are used as great tools to understand, expose and criticize the objectification process of women. The texts that are most helpful for feminists who want to use Sartre this way are *Being and Nothingness* and *Anti-Semite and Jew*. As Julien S. Murphy puts it, "These two texts, so centered on freedom and oppression, resonate with feminist theories of liberation" (Murphy, 8).

It seems, from this description, that the male human being takes on the project of making being be through its sexual activity, which consists of sacrificing his flesh to plug up holes. The female human being, in contrast, merely awaits such filling and wishes to capture the male flesh. This hardly makes for a harmonious relation among human beings and is bound to reinforce the view that concrete relations with others are conflictual.

THE PROBLEM OF ETHICS

It appears that interpersonal relations are, indeed, essentially conflictual. The way Sartre has explained the situation, the Other's upsurge in my world alienates me—the Other is a threat to me. This is also true of intimate relationships such as love and sexual relations. If it is true that the for-itself engages in relations with others with the intention to master or destroy the freedom of the Other, in order to free itself from the alienating consciousness of the Other, how is ethics possible? If all that exists is a struggle between consciousnesses, an ethics of freedom and authenticity seems to be impossible. Remember that Sartre has said that the for-itself must strive toward authenticity. Part of it, as he will discuss it in the *Notebooks for an Ethics*, involves willing the freedom of the Other. Further, although Sartre does not propose rules of conduct, he does speak of a fundamental value: freedom. Any ethical decision must be made in view of freedom and its promotion. I have to aim at acting freely, but I must also aim at fostering the freedom of others. But to me, willing the freedom of the Other means willing my own alienation, which is not particularly conducive to authenticity. It seems that we are caught in a circle, or are we?

In fact, it is only later in his writings that Sartre successfully comes to terms with an ethics of freedom that truly entails willing the Other as free. In his existentialist period, the focus remains on the individual's own striving for authenticity, i.e. one's acknowledgment of one's freedom. In the next chapters, we will see how Sartre's views evolve gradually and lead him to embrace commitment in not only literature but also in politics—a politics of liberation that aims at the freedom of all.

SUMMARY

I am not alone in the world: there are others. When I encounter the Other, I feel alienated as the Other knows me as an object in his world. I can never experience myself the way the Other experiences me. Thus, the Other is said to know a secret about me. The analysis of the look allows Sartre to explain how the presence of an Other radically and fundamentally affects my world and my self. Because I am objectified by the Other and feel alienated, relations with others will be tainted: conflict is the essence of our relations with others. To Sartre, "Hell is other people!" Even love—the one relation we might think to be safe from conflict—does not fare well. In love, we attempt to capture the Other's freedom, in order to escape alienation. Sartre's views on gender and sexual relations are no more positive, with a stereotypical view that opposes the sexes. Sartre's rather negative views on interpersonal relations pose a problem for the elaboration of an ethics.

6

ETHICS AND THE
HUMAN CONDITION

It is time for us to pause and weave together the different ideas we have explored. Sartre's views are complex, and it is not easy to disentangle them from one another. The multiple cross-referencing from chapter to chapter probably gave you a sense of that. This chapter brings all of those ideas together and further discusses the problem of ethics that faces Sartre given the nature of his existentialist philosophy as delineated in his writings of the 1940s.

SARTRE'S WRITINGS ON ETHICS

It is first in the public lecture "Existentialism Is a Humanism" that Sartre tackles ethical questions as unfolding from his ontological positions described in *Being and Nothingness*. Remember that he closes this treatise by promising to devote his next work to the development of an ethics: "All these questions, which refer us to a pure and not an accessory reflection, can find their reply only on the ethical plane. We shall devote to them a future work" (BN 798). This promise, however, remained unfulfilled. Sartre wrote the *Notebooks for an Ethics* from 1947 to 1948, and then abandoned it. Two of the 10 notebooks that he filled were published posthumously in 1983. Sartre said, about his abandonment of the project of an ethics at the end of the 1940s, that "I have written 10 big notebooks that represent a failed attempt at an ethics. [...] I have not finished because ... it is tough to devise an ethics!" (my translation of "J'ai rédigé une dizaine de gros cahiers de notes qui représentent une tentative *manquée* pour une morale. [...] Je n'ai pas achevé parce que ... c'est difficile à faire une morale!" (Sartre et Sicard, "Entretien. L'écriture et la publication" 14). Again, in the 1960s, Sartre attempted to elaborate an ethics. The result is two sets of elaborated notes, one for a conference he gave in April 1964 in Rome, the other for a series of conferences that he was going to pronounce at Cornell University in April 1965 (he did not go to Cornell, explaining that he had withdrawn in protest against the American involvement in Vietnam). The latter set of notes (Rome and Cornell) present a "dialectical ethics" that still revolves around the notion of freedom.

I will thus revisit the important notions of freedom, responsibility, anguish, situatedness, the existence of the Other, and alienation. I will also re-examine the ethical ideal of authenticity that emerges from Sartre's views. I will delineate how Sartre's thought shifts with the abandonment of the *Notebooks for an Ethics*, the writing of *What Is Literature?*, and his embracing of commitment. We will then be in a position to move to the following chapters, which discuss at length Sartre's notion of commitment and his views on politics.

THE SITUATED HUMAN BEING

As we have seen earlier, to Sartre, I am conscious, I exist. I exist as a consciousness thrown into the world. No one put me there: there is no God who planned this, no overarching meaning to my presence in the world. In fact, I am the one giving meaning to the world through my interaction with being. An embodied consciousness, I go about the world and interpret it. All the while, I project myself and give my life meaning. All of my actions and decisions are made in light of the project I have of my self. All acts contribute to give meaning to this project, to make it happen. This is all possible because I am a free consciousness. I exist as a freedom that unfolds in the world. Sartre insists that my freedom is absolute: I am not determined in any way, I do not have an essence and I am free to make myself. At the same time that he insists on my being free, Sartre claims that this absolute freedom entails an equally absolute responsibility. I am the one making myself, and I have to assume responsibility for my choices. I am entirely responsible for myself and always truly the author of my deeds. As we have seen, though, it will ever be tempting for me to flee my own responsibility by embracing bad faith (see Chapter 4).

If the self I have chosen is a morally flawed one, for example, I would much rather blame everybody and everything else but me. I am thus always tempted, in bad faith, to believe that something else made me what I am, that I was obeying a transcendent order of values (something Sartre rejects along with the existence of God). The waiter in the café (whom we discussed in Chapter 4), for example, plays at being a waiter. He lies to himself about his freedom, and pretends that he has no choice but behave as he does: he faithfully plays a role that has been determined for him and not by him. You will remember that Sartre goes so far as to say that we are always in bad faith—even while we are in good faith since good faith, too, is a lie to oneself! As we said then, this poses a problem for an ethics like that of Sartre, which emphasizes the importance of authenticity.

I am a free consciousness in the world. This consciousness is embodied. That body is the facticity of my being. It determines me somewhat insofar as I have not chosen it. I exist as a consciousness and female body with all of its particularities. While I have not chosen that body that I am, I may choose—thanks to my absolute freedom—the meaning that this body has for me and thus how I exist it in the world. Likewise, I am born in a situation that I have not chosen, but I may choose the meaning this situation has for me. If I have a disability, it is I who give it the meaning I want; if I am born in a destitute milieu, it is still I who decide on the meaning of that socioeconomic situation.

The world is populated by others. As we saw in Chapter 5, the presence of the Other is alienating for me. The Other steals the world away from me: he knows a secret about me, objectifies me and attempts either to seduce and captivate my freedom or to control and crush it. The fact that others exist is a fundamental aspect of the human being's situation. No individual can escape the conflictual encounter with the Other. The question of how one can opt for an ethical stance on one's life is pressing, especially given the threat that the Other poses. Is it possible to work toward authenticity and freedom for oneself without the Other being somehow involved?

As we have seen, the situation of the human being seems pretty anguishing: I am entirely responsible for myself, I am thrown into the world, left to myself; my presence and the world are completely contingent. The presence of the Other is also contingent and yet alienating to me. It almost looks like I might be better off if I was not free and lied to myself, even if only just a bit. That, however, is not Sartre's opinion; he thinks that it is our moral duty to actualize our freedom and to come to terms with our "condition."

ANGUISH REDUX!

Many of Sartre's literary characters are very good examples of persons dealing with anguish and submerged in bad faith. Some others are very lucid about their condition and present themselves as existential heroes of freedom. We have met a few in the previous chapters. Roquentin is one who discovers the contingency of existence including his own. Suffering from nausea, he understands what kind of being he is, and what he needs to do to escape bad faith and be the master of his life. His choice for justifying his otherwise unjustifiable presence in the world: creating values by writing a novel. Before coming to this "existential revelation," Roquentin is anguished and feels a complete loss of meaning. Sartre's powerful descriptions of Roquentin's anguish and despair illustrate the human plight. The conclusion of the novel is also indicative of the path each individual ought to take.

Goetz, the main character of the play *The Devil and the Good Lord*, similarly opts for the creation of values, albeit in a different, more pragmatic way. We discussed in Chapter 2 how he embraces atheism, freedom, and human responsibility. Likewise Mathieu, in the trilogy *The Roads of Freedom*, realizes that he must take responsibility for his acts. After years of attempting to be a detached, non-committed freedom, he sees that a freedom that is not anchored in the world and does not take responsibility for itself is flawed. In the play *The Flies*, Orestes is a very lucid character. He understands that he is absolutely free and entirely responsible, and he acts accordingly.

These characters all emerge from the period during which Sartre is presenting his view of the anguished freedom. All of these characters illustrate, in their own way, that despair and anguish are not the final words of Sartre's philosophy. Rather, an authentic attitude is possible and ethics is a viable project. We will understand this better by looking closely at Sartre's last original play.

IS AUTHENTICITY POSSIBLE? THE CASE OF FRANTZ

While Goetz and Orestes are living the death of God to the fullest, the character of Frantz in *The Condemned of Altona* is unable to confront his own responsibility. He is sequestered in that he denies his own freedom and relentlessly makes himself accountable to a tribunal of crabs, the inhabitants of the 30th century who replace the absent God. He is sequestered mentally and physically, living his whole life in his room: he lives in bad faith.

THE CONDEMNED OF ALTONA

First staged in 1959 and published in 1960, the play presents the story of the von Guerlach family in Altona, near Hamburg. The action takes place in the family house where the son, Frantz, lives locked into his room. Everyone thinks he died during World War II, and everybody pretends it is the case. Only the father and Frantz's sister know of his self-imposed sequestration. Frantz only ever sees one person, his sister, with whom he has incestuous relations. The play unfolds after the father announces that he is about to die. His daughter-in-law seeks to find the truth about Frantz and succeeds in meeting him in his room, passing herself off as his sister. As the play continues and Frantz unveils some of his secrets, the audience understands that he is crushed by guilt from a deed he committed during the war: as an officer of the *Wehrmacht* on the Russian front, he tortured two partisans in order to save his own men. At the end of the play, Frantz commits suicide with his father.

Frantz likes to believe that he has been made what he is. He thinks that his father, his family, his position in the army, and his participation in the war have made him what he is. He says: "One does not make war: war makes us" (Condemned 287; my translation). This is what he aims to believe while he is trying to justify his actions. Further, he claims:

> But I never choose, my dear girl! I am chosen. Nine months before my birth they had chosen my name, my career, my character, and my fate. I tell you that this prison routine has been forced upon me, and you should understand that I would not submit myself to it unless it was vitally necessary.

(Condemned 84)

Despite his efforts at denying his freedom, it remains that Frantz is a free being: after all, he freely imposes upon himself his sequestration. It is also freely that he creates his tribunal of crabs.

Toward the end of the play, Frantz admits his own responsibility. He abandons bad faith and embraces his past deeds as his own. True enough, his situation shaped him to a certain extent, but, at the moment of choice, he was free. Interestingly, we can even say that his suicide, at the end of the play, is a confirmation of this. Frantz finally succeeds in being authentic. He realizes that he made himself what he is and that he was free all the time and not determined to anything. Realizing this, he also acknowledges his responsibility for his deeds. Because these are unforgivable, he comes to the conclusion that he must commit suicide. His deeds are unforgivable because they have destroyed the freedom of others. Frantz is free and responsible. He is the only judge, he deems himself guilty, and he executes himself. When Sartre works on his ethics in the *Notebooks for an Ethics*, he warns that his ethics will be tough. The case of Frantz shows that authenticity is possible, but it is also possible that one will be unable to face oneself, or that the only possible good that one can do is to freely condemn oneself.

Frantz is a very different character than Orestes and Goetz. But the ethics of these characters (as well as those of the characters of Sartre's other plays) is one of freedom. Sartre's theater presents us with characters in situation. This is very interesting, as one of the problems we identified has to do with what looks like the abstractness of situation in the face of freedom as absolute. Sartre's characters are absolute freedoms, but they have to act as situated beings. In an interview for *France Nouvelle*, Sartre says the following about Frantz and the other characters of the play: "For me, the world makes man and man makes the world. I did not want to merely put characters on stage, rather, I wanted to suggest that objective circumstances condition the shaping and behavior of this or that individual at a certain given time" (my translation of "Pour moi, le monde fait l'homme et l'homme fait le monde. Je n'ai pas voulu seulement mettre en scène des caractères, mais suggérer que des circonstances objectives conditionnent la formation et le comportement de tel ou tel individu, à un moment donné" (Théâtre 365). It looks as if, at least in this later play, Sartre recognizes the weight of situation more than he did in his earlier writings. We will return to this.

Whether freedom is absolute or situated is not important for us to determine that an ethics of freedom requires that one be authentic. This is illustrated in Sartre's theater. Further, his plays show that even if the individual will face anguish and the temptation of bad faith, authenticity is indeed always possible.

FREEDOM AND AUTHENTICITY OR BUST!

We saw in Chapter 3 that there has been an important evolution in Sartre's thought, from an early notion of absolute freedom to a later notion of situated freedom. The key to his ethical thinking throughout all periods of his life remains the notion of freedom. One is born a free consciousness, and one's existence is a struggle to make oneself free. It is one thing to be free ontologically and another to be able to recognize oneself as such. It is yet another matter to be able to exercise one's freedom practically. In the ethical realm, the notion of freedom becomes the absolute value for Sartre. We have seen in Chapter 4 that the moral exigency that emerges in his writings is the striving for authenticity. One ought to be authentic, but, as we have seen, this striving is exactly the attempt, on the part of the individual, to acknowledge his/her freedom. Freedom and authenticity are thus intertwined.

One must aim to be free and thus authentic. The difficulty, as we have indicated earlier, is twofold: first, the anguish before one's freedom makes bad faith very tempting; second, the presence of the Other in the world is a threat to one's freedom. So even if one jumps the first hurdle, it seems the second is even more daunting. As we said in Chapter 5, Sartre's forceful descriptions of interpersonal relationships as conflictual do not bode well for an ethics of freedom. This is Sartre's position in *Being and Nothingness*. However, starting with the *Notebooks for an Ethics*, he begins to present things in a different way.

THE NEED FOR THE OTHER

Sartre has made very clear in his earlier writings that the individual free consciousness is responsible for creating meaning and interpreting the world. However, if I am doing this by myself, my world and the meaning I give to it are absolutely contingent—they are not justified in any way. Sartre argues in the *Notebooks* that I can only make my presence in the world necessary, and provide some foundation to my world and the meaning I give it, through the intervention of the Other. He says in *Being and Nothingness* that the essence of my relation to the Other is conflict, but he also says: "For me the Other is first the being for whom I am an object; that is the being *through whom* I gain my objectness" (BN 361). The Other objectifies me; I am an object for him. This can be negative, but it is also positive as he will later emphasize in the *Notebooks*. There he says: "Through the Other I am enriched in a new dimension of Being: through the Other I come to exist in the dimension of Being, through the Other I become an object" (Notebooks 499). I am anguished by my own freedom and I am seeking to be grounded in the world, to be a necessary being. The Other, who objectifies me, can do that for me. He can be a "savior" in that my being and the values I choose may be fixed in the world by his objectifying look. So instead of fleeing the Other, I should actively appeal to him so that he chooses my values and my being as part of his world.

Sartre makes clear that I need the Other in order to exist authentically and freely. He says:

> The Other, through his active recognition of the instrumentality of the world (that is, in making use of it), breaks the cycle of immanence. I am necessary as the foundation of the instrumentality of the world that is necessary to the Other. And more exactly I become the instrumentality of the world. I am a foundation in my being in the world insofar as the Other grasps it as being-for-him.
>
> (Notebooks 540)

What Sartre is saying here is this: the Other grasps a world and gives it meaning for himself. I am an object in that world. If the Other acknowledges my presence in his world, then my presence, my acts, the values I have chosen, all become objects in his world. They are justified and grounded by another consciousness. It is only if the Other is free that he can do that; only a free consciousness can give meaning to a world and acknowledge the presence of others in it. This will entail that I must work actively to make the Other, as well as myself, free.

The key to this is the acknowledgment of freedom in oneself and in the Other. The Other is in the world in the same way that I am. When I am an object in the world of the Other and:

> If […] he makes me exist as an existing freedom as well as a *Being/object*, if
> he makes this autonomous moment exist and thematizes this contingency that
> I perpetually surpass, he enriches the world and me, he *gives a meaning* to my
> existence *in addition* to the subjective meaning I myself give it […]
>
> (Notebooks 500)

I can give meaning to my existence and my world all I want but if the
Other contributes to it by his own existence and acknowledgment of
mine, then I stand on firmer ground.

Consciousness gives meaning to being and rescues it from absurdity
(as we discussed in Chapter 1), but I still need the Other to objectify
and affirm this meaning. The Other thus complements my self, and
validates the justification and meaning that I have created. He does so
only if he is made free, and only if he decides to respond to my
appeal. The problem is this: how does one coerce a free Other to
acknowledge another free consciousness, given that one is then at the
mercy of that free consciousness? The answer is this: it is also to the
Other's advantage to acknowledge my free being. The Other is also
seeking justification and objectification. It is a trade-off: you acknowledge me, I acknowledge you. Simone de Beauvoir explored these ideas
in her *Pyrrhus and Cinéas* (1944). In this essay, she argues that a person
alone in the world would be paralyzed by the futility of all their goals.
We are not alone in the world and others are there whom we can
appeal to. Beauvoir explains that I have to make of others my "fellow
men […] in order for our appeals not to be lost in the void, there
must be men ready to hear me close by, and these men must be my
peers" (*Philosophical Writings* 137). A peer is one who is recognized as
a free consciousness. Thomas C. Anderson sums it up:

> since God is dead, as are all objective values, man is completely dependent on
> the freedom of men if he is to attain meaning and value for his existence. Man
> fundamentally desires a justified existence and the knowledge that it is justi-
> fied, and this means he wants to be freely and positively valued by all men,
> whom he wants to be his peers. Consistency demands, therefore, that man
> both value the freedom of all men and aid them in becoming his equals.
>
> (Anderson, *The Foundation and Structure of Sartrean Ethics* 89)

The view presented in the *Notebooks for an Ethics* is significantly different from that presented in *Being and Nothingness*. Why did Sartre

abandon the ethics project in the *Notebooks*? Did he think that it was too important a shift in his thinking? Did he think that it was impossible to go from conflict with, to conversion to, the Other? There is another way to argue for the conversion to the Other, and that is by an examination of freedom as fundamental value.

AN ETHICS OF FREEDOM

Sartre's whole philosophy revolves around the central notion of freedom. His ethics holds it as its fundamental value and posits an ideal of authenticity as the flourishing of the individual as a freedom. Sartre's ethics can thus be said to aim at the flourishing of the individual, a flourishing that will be possible once the individual recognizes himself and others as free. Taking the human individual's flourishing as its goal, Sartre's ethics is humanistic: it focuses on the human individual and it rejects the existence of any transcendent realm or values (we discussed Sartre's atheism in Chapter 2).

Sartre's ethics does not focus on rules of conduct; it does not propose any ethical rule or guideline that one should follow in decision-making. Rather, it leaves the individual to himself to choose values. This contributes to the anguish one may already feel in the face of one's freedom. In *Existentialism is a Humanism*, Sartre discusses the example of the young student who sought advice from him. During the war, a young man was faced with the option of staying in Paris to assist his mother or going to England to join the Résistance. He asked Sartre for advice. Sartre's answer was:

> You're free, choose, that is, invent. No general ethics can show you what is to be done; there are no omens in the world. The Catholics will reply, "But there are." Granted—but *in any case, I myself choose the meaning they have*.
>
> (EH 28, emphasis added)

Further, he explains that by deciding to consult Sartre, rather than someone else, he had already made a choice. Given his existentialist position, Sartre can only leave him to himself to decide what to do and, in any case, whatever advice he could dare offer to the young man will be subject to the young man's free choice or refusal.

Beauvoir has said of existentialist ethics that it "does not furnish recipes any more than do science and art. One can merely propose methods" (Beauvoir, *The Ethics of Ambiguity* 134). This also applies to what Sartre has to offer, but that does not mean that no guiding principle exists. In fact, there is one fundamental principle that one can use to guide one's moral life: the respect and promotion of freedom. We could formulate the following principle on the basis of all that we have examined in Sartre's philosophy so far: all that affirms, respects and promotes freedom is good; all that negates and destroys it is bad. Each individual is left to themselves to decide what this means in terms of concrete actions. Faced with a decision to help my neighbor or not, I must decide, for myself, which action is the most conducive to the promotion of freedom. This will not always be easy, but it is all I can do. One cannot expect from Sartre (or anyone, for that matter) a precise guideline for conduct. The individual is free— free to choose, free to give meaning, free to promote freedom for himself and others, or even free not to. All rests on the individual's freedom. Because this is the case, there is no absolute moral obligation other than the one that the individual would posit for him/herself.

IMPLICATIONS

To be authentic and to actualize oneself as a freedom, the individual needs to work actively toward the freedom of others. This implies that the individual must surpass the ontological conflict between consciousnesses. Is this possible? A few literary characters show that it is and that the fundamental moral principle is indeed applicable. Mathieu, in *The Roads to Freedom*, ends up converting to the Other by committing himself. In *The Flies*, Orestes' decision to free the people of Argos by making the flies follow him is an act that promotes the freedom of others. In *The Condemned of Altona*, Frantz condemns himself because he has violated the fundamental principle and destroyed other freedoms. Goetz makes himself free. But what of Roquentin's choice at the end of *Nausea*?

You will remember that Roquentin was suffering from nausea because nothing had meaning any more (see Chapter 1). To cure himself, Roquentin has to find a way to justify his presence in the world and to fix meaning on things. Every time he hears his favorite song played in the café where he hangs out, the world makes sense for him. Reflecting on this experience, he realizes that the composer and the singer are justified, that they have "washed themselves of the sin of existing" (N 177). For his part, and throughout the novel, Roquentin has been working on the biography of an historical character, M. de Rollebon. He decides to abandon this project and instead opts for writing a piece of literature, probably a novel. This is the decision he has taken as he is about to leave Bouville at the end of *Nausea*.

This is an ethical choice, and it is one that promotes Roquentin's freedom, as well as that of others. As we will see in the next chapter, the writer's activity is one that appeals to the freedom of his reader. Committed literature is one way for the individual to flourish as an authentic individual that acknowledges himself and others as free and that works actively at making the Others his peers.

SUMMARY

The picture that Sartre draws of the human condition is not heavenly, to say the least. The individual is thrown into a world where he is entirely free and responsible for himself. As a result, he will be anguished. But authenticity requires that he embraces this situation. Authenticity is possible, according to Sartre. The individual is also thrown into a world where he is in conflict with the others he encounters. This creates difficulties for ethics but, as Sartre shows in his *Notebooks*, conversion to the Other is both required and possible: I need the Other to justify my pursuits. The ethics that emerges from that picture is an ethics of freedom that posits authenticity as its ideal and freedom as its fundamental value. We ought always, therefore, to act in such a way as to respect and promote freedom in ourselves and in others.

7

COMMITTED LITERATURE

Sartre's thinking about freedom evolved through his writings as he tackled certain problems that arose from his conception of absolute freedom. One major change had to do with his increased recognition of the power of situation. Recognizing this, he rethought the role of the writer in effecting social change. As a writer himself, Sartre saw that he had a particular social and political role to play.

I will explain how Sartre's war experience, and his discovery of historicity, led him to this idea. From an attempt at direct political engagement in the resistance that was ultimately unsuccessful, Sartre moved to another form of engagement as a writer. I will look into the theory of committed literature that is exposed in *What Is Literature?* (1947). This will be accompanied by an explanation of how Sartre himself adopted this view and how it transformed his own writings. He wanted literature to have a "real" effect in the world, and conceived of it as an appeal to the reader's freedom. I will also discuss *Les Temps modernes* venture and how it was meant to represent the new role literature was taking on.

A TRANSFORMATIVE WAR EXPERIENCE

In September 1939, Sartre was drafted into the French army to serve as a soldier in a meteorological unit. Beauvoir, who had kept a diary throughout her life, convinced Sartre to take on this activity. We talked about this in relation to the concept of authenticity in Chapter 4. In the meteorological unit, his duties took only a small amount of time, leaving Sartre with a lot of time to read and write. The *War Diaries* (1939–40) are a mixture of diary writing and philosophical reflections, with many of their pages considered to be early drafts for *Being and Nothingness*. Some of these reflections include thinking about his own situation as an individual drafted in a war that was not of his own making. He did not choose to make war—he would rather have had peace—but the fact is he was drafted and ended up participating in a war that was not of his own choosing. After much reflection, Sartre concluded that this war *was* his war: "The war is me. It is my being-in-the-world, it is the world-for-me" (my translation, Carnets 101).

Thinking about his own situation allowed Sartre to uncover his own historicity [he says: "The war unveiled my historicity" (Carnets 160)] and, de facto, the fundamental fact that human beings are historical and factical beings, situated in the world. While his character had not changed, his situation had indeed been radically altered. This means that his being was changed, since the situation makes the individual. Thinking about his being-at-war led Sartre to reevaluate his political positions. Up to the war, he had been an "apolitical anarchist" with socialist leanings. The war made him realize that because one is situated, and because one is a part of the historical process and may transform and shape it by one's own actions and choices, it is crucial that one be committed and actively take upon oneself this sociohistoric becoming. To not choose is still to make a choice, but a better choice is to choose and be committed, which is what he decided for himself. He says:

> One sees clearly that war is of a different order. I think that it is amongst the grand irrationals, such as birth, death, misery, suffering, among which each man is thrown and in the face of which to abstain is still to commit oneself.
>
> (Carnets 136)

His commitment took different forms during the war. His first, and lifelong, commitment was to write. As a prisoner in the POW camp, Sartre wrote, staged, and acted in the play *Bariona*, a mystery play on the birth of Christ that conveyed an implicit message of hope for the prisoners of the camp. As Boulé notes, "Sartre has changed [...] It is as if he is accepting his historical situation. [...] Sartre is absolutely not miserable. And what is he doing? Writing ... " (Boulé: *Sartre*, 120). Sartre recounted his work on *Bariona*, how much he enjoyed acting in the plays staged in the camp, and reassured Beauvoir: "My Love, I am not bored at all, I am really cheerful." (*Lettres au Castor II* 300). He was discovering, at the time, the power of theater and his skills as a playwright. Analyzing *Bariona*, Sartre has claimed that, however flawed a play it was, *Bariona* was a way of communicating with his fellow soldiers and talking about their own captivity in the face of the German authorities. All the latter saw in it was a Christmas mystery play, whereas the prisoners understood it as conveying a political message of liberation. What is important here is the enthusiasm Sartre felt about theater, starting with the writing and performance of *Bariona*. He says to Beauvoir: "But you should know that I certainly have talent as a playwright [...]" (Lettres au Castor II 300). The performance of the play made Sartre realize how powerful a communication tool theater could be, a realization that led him to adopt play-writing thereafter as one of his favored modes of expression. Situational theater is a tool for communicating with audiences that can be as effective as literature (we will see in the section on committed literature how Sartre conceives of literature as commitment).

SARTRE AS RÉSISTANT

When he was released from the POW camp and returned to Paris, Sartre felt an urge to get involved and join the Résistance. Beauvoir was startled by this radical change at first but she too soon embarked on the adventure. Sartre founded "Socialisme et liberté" in the spring of 1941, a resistance group that was also a think-tank for the future.

SOCIALISME ET LIBERTÉ

This group, formed on Sartre's initiative, joined together Marxists and non-Marxists, including the likes of Simone de Beauvoir, Maurice Merleau-Ponty, and other famed alumni of École Normale Supérieure. They published clandestine pamphlets. Dominique Desanti has explained in many interviews that the dynamic was special: the editorial of their bulletin would be written once by a Marxist and once by a non-Marxist, etc. The non-Marxist was Sartre. It is interesting to note that although he had not started "flirting" with Marxism at the time (which we will see more of in Chapter 8), Sartre had a very open attitude, and let the Marxists of the group express their own views—an openness that was not usual in other similar groups. This may have been due to his recently acquired political sensibility.

He went on a bicycle trip in the free zone of France along with Beauvoir to meet with writers André Gide (1869–1951) and André Malraux (1901–76), in an effort to connect his small group to the larger resistance movement. Despite Sartre's wishes to be active in the resistance, his participation therein was very limited. Here is how Beauvoir described their situation in occupied Paris:

> Politically, we found ourselves reduced to a condition of total impotence. When Sartre started 'Socialism and Liberty' he hoped this group would attach itself to a much larger central body; but our trip had produced no very important results, and our return to Paris proved no less disappointing. Already the various movements that had sprung up right at the beginning were disbanded or in the process of breaking up. Like ours, they had come into being through individual initiative, and consisted mainly of middle-class intellectuals without any experience of underground action—or indeed of action in any form.
>
> (Beauvoir, *The Prime of Life*, 499)

Despite this "failed" attempt at being a résistant, Sartre should be given credit for having tried to do something while others were content with inaction. From our point of view as readers of Sartre's philosophy and literature, this "failure" may even be considered a good thing in the end, considering the activity that Sartre took up as a result. His reaction to the group's lack of success and to the adversity surrounding him in occupied Paris, and its "Nazification," was to lead him to take up his pen and write *Being and Nothingness* and *The Flies*. Indeed, Annie Cohen-Solal sees the increasing repression exercised by the occupant in 1942 as the soil from which these works grew. As citizens of Paris were increasingly deprived of their rights, Sartre "resisted" and wrote a philosophical treatise and a play on absolute freedom (see Cohen-Solal, *Jean-Paul Sartre: A Life*). David Drake explains that at the liberation, Sartre was regarded as a symbol of intellectual resistance:

He had written for the underground resistance press and had fooled the
German censors into allowing him to present *The Flies* in the capital, a play
hailed by the Communist paper *Action* as a model of 'resistance theater' [...]

(Drake 61)

However, as Sartre would put it later, he was more of a writer who
resisted than a resistant who wrote! John Gerassi comments that
"from 1945 on, Sartre did more than any other intellectual in the
world to denounce injustice and to support the wretched of the earth"
(Gerassi 187).

A COMMITTED WRITER: *LES TEMPS MODERNES*

Sartre's notion of commitment arose during the war, and was put to
work not only in his own writings but also in the journal he launched
in 1945, *Les Temps modernes* (borrowing the title of Charlie Chaplin's
famous movie, *Modern Times* [1936]). The first issue, published in
October 1945, contains a text by Sartre simply titled "Présentation."
In it, Sartre explained what the journal's aims were but he also began
to sketch a theory of literature and the role that writers have to
assume—a theory that would find its full-blown expression in the
essay *What is Literature?* in 1947.

What must the writer be? Writers must be committed individuals
and their commitment is their writing. Sartre begins the presentation
by criticizing bourgeois writers who failed to play their social role.
Writers such as Honoré de Balzac (1799–1850) and Gustave Flaubert
were indifferent to the world around them and the social changes that
were either occurring or needed. They wrote but they failed to
account for the world in which they lived. In this, they were not truly
situated individuals. They attempted—in bad faith—to dissociate
themselves from their situation. They failed to accomplish their mis-
sions for themselves and for others. Sartre thought that the lack of
commitment on the part of nineteenth-century writers brought some
confusion about the role of literature. He ironized and said: "Today,
things are at the point where we have seen some writers, blamed or
punished because they had rented their pen to the Germans, display a
painful surprise. 'What?' they say, 'so what one writes commits oneself?'" (my translation of "'Aujourd'hui, les choses en sont venues à ce

point que l'on a vu des écrivains, blamés ou punis parce qu'ils ont loué leur plume aux Allemands, faire montre d'un étonnement douloureux. 'Eh quoi? disent-ils, ça engage donc ce qu'on écrit?'" ["Présentation des Temps modernes"]).

To Sartre, it is clear that one's writings are a commitment. In the essay introducing *Les Temps modernes*, he explains that every piece of writing has a meaning, whether it conforms to its author's intent or not. The writer is responsible for the meaning of the piece he has created. The writer is a situated individual and therefore must embrace his situation. This corresponds to the ethical requirement for authenticity that Sartre had already spelled out. Passivity and indifference are still ways for one to be in the world. They are options, but options that do not make the most of the situation of the individual. The writer who does not comment on his world is one who withdraws from it. His silence is a statement, even if it is a negative one. It remains a way for the writer to account for the world. Is it acceptable then? Not according to Sartre, who thought that there is a responsibility for the writer, one he had learned during the occupation: since one is in the world and therefore acts upon it even while not desiring to, it is preferable to make of this action a voluntary impact. One must will one's impact on the world. As a writer, one's impact is brought about through what one writes. One must fully be engaged in accounting for the world in one's writing, and one must take full responsibility for one's writings.

Not only must the writer take responsibility for his writings, but he must also try to bring about change. That is what Sartre identifies as the task of the new journal he is launching:

We side with those who wish to change both the social condition of man and the way he sees himself. Thus, our journal will take a position regarding every political and social event to come. It will not do so politically, by which I mean it won't serve any party, but it will try to unveil the conception of man underlying the various theses and it will give its opinion on these conceptions. […] we will be happy that literature will fulfill, once again, what it should always have been: a social role.

(My translation of "nous nous rangeons du côté de ceux qui veulent changer à la fois la condition sociale de l'homme et la conception qu'il a de lui-même. Aussi, à propos des événements politiques et sociaux qui viennent, notre revue prendra position en chaque cas. Elle ne le fera pas politiquement, c'est-à-dire qu'elle ne servira aucun parti; mais elle s'efforcera de dégager la conception de l'homme dont s'inspireront les thèses en présence et elle donnera son avis

conformément à la conception qu'elle soutient. [...] nous nous féliciterons
[que] la littérature soit redevenue ce qu'elle n'aurait jamais dû cesser d'être:
une fonction sociale." [Présentation 16].)

What is lurking here is a view of politics that puts writing on a
different level than mere party allegiance and support. Concrete politics rests upon philosophical conceptions of the world and of the
human being. The task of the journal, then, would be to go beyond a
surface understanding of the political to that deeper and broader
politics. Each concrete event to be commented upon would be the
occasion for the writers involved in the journal to take a position and
unveil the fundamental principles at work. This is a task that writers
must undertake, and the journal that will offer this to its readers
within its pages will do so with the aim of changing the world and
liberating individuals. Again, the fundamental principle at work here is
that of freedom, and its goal is liberation.

Sartre explains that this goal is a long-term one:

> Since man is a totality, it is not enough, in effect, to grant him the right to vote
> without addressing the other factors that constitute him. He must free himself
> totally, that is, he must make himself other, in acting upon his biological con-
> stitution as much as upon his economic conditioning, upon his sexual com-
> plexes as much as upon the political givens of his situation.
>
> [my translation of "Puisque l'homme est une totalité, il ne sufit pas, en effet,
> de lui accorder le droit de vote, sans toucher aux autres facteurs qui le con-
> stituent. Il faut qu'il se délivre totalement, c'est-à-dire qu'il se fasse autre, en
> agissant sur sa constitution biologique aussi bien que sur son conditionnement
> économique, sur ses complexes sexuels aussi bien que sur les données poli-
> tiques de sa situation" [Présentation].)

Here, Sartre introduces the distinction between concrete politics
and a more fundamental political approach. In order to liberate human
beings, to make them free, it is important that one addresses all parts
of their lives. The liberation of individuals thus requires a well-roun-
ded approach. The writer can contribute by providing accounts of the
situation, analyses of the way in which the situation impedes freedom,
and what can be done to fix it. Sartre argues that the individual is
total: "Totally committed and totally free. It is nonetheless the free
man that we must free, in broadening his possibilities for choice." [my

translation of "Totalement engagé et totalement libre. C'est pourtant cet homme libre qu'il faut délivrer, en élargissant ses possibilités de choix" ["Présentation des Temps modernes"]). *Les Temps modernes* would have as a goal to defend individual autonomy, to broaden the possibilities for choice and thus to protect and generate more freedom.

While Sartre did not articulate in this short essay the reason why the writer must be committed and must attend to the sociopolitical reality of his world, it can be reconstructed and we have the tools for that from the previous chapters. Having looked at Sartre's views on freedom, authenticity and an ethics of freedom, we can identify the philosophical foundation for the claims he presents. These are also at work in the essay *What Is Literature?*

COMMITTED LITERATURE

While he was working on the third volume of *The Roads to Freedom* and on his ethics, Sartre wrote and published *What Is Literature?* in 1947. Sartre had been drawn to literature from an early age, and had been a writer for many years prior to setting out to write this theoretical reflection on the nature of literature. In it, he discussed the role of the writer and defended the view that literature must be committed. The writer is a free being, but his freedom is best exercised through commitment. We saw that Sartre's war experience was the occasion for him to discover that. For Sartre, as a human being, the writer is a situated being, i.e. a situated freedom, as he had argued in his presentation of *Les Temps modernes*. In *What Is Literature?*, he investigates the relationship between the writer and the reader, and argues that the writer is talking to likewise situated readers. This "dialogue" between freedoms is a situated, historical, and factical one. Genuine dialogue can only happen if commitment happens. For commitment to happen, one must let one's freedom be tied to one's situation. In *What Is Literature?* then, the moral exigency to make oneself free is slightly transformed: one must make oneself a situated freedom.

The essay is structured in three sections, asking fundamental questions about literature: What is writing? Why write? For whom does one write? A fourth section, which addresses the situation of the writer in 1947, completes the essay. In his foreword, Sartre points out: "It seems that nobody ever asked himself these questions" (WL viii).

He begins by distinguishing writing from other aesthetic endeavours and by distinguishing prose from poetry. The writer deals with significations. Sartre explains: "The empire of signs is prose; poetry is on the side of painting, sculpture and music" (WL 4). He thus wants to distinguish the two types of writing, and he focuses his analysis on prose. The writer of prose uses words with a purpose, he speaks to his reader. His speech is action of a particular kind. Sartre explains:

> The prose-writer is a man who has chosen a certain method of secondary action which we may call action by disclosure. [...] The "engaged" writer knows that words are action. He knows that to reveal is to change and that one can reveal only by planning to change.
>
> (WL 14)

The writer's speech is deeply transformative because it is an unveiling. Using words, the writer shows the world and human beings to the reader, so that the reader "may assume full responsibility before the object which has thus been laid bare" (WL 15). The writer's role is tremendously important: he must unveil the world to the reader so that the reader feels responsible for the world and wants to improve it. The writer's role is "to act in such a way that nobody can be ignorant of the world and that nobody may say that he is innocent of what it's all about". The reader who is confronted with the real world in his readings cannot pretend to be unaware of the problems in it. Being aware, he must act to change the world. This ties back to the notion of willing the Other as free so that I may be free. As a reader, I may be confronted with the fact that individual freedoms are impinged upon. Because I long to be free, I need the greatest number of people to be free. It becomes my duty to act in such a way that these individuals are made free. My own longing for freedom entails that I take concrete measures to make the world one in which I and others may be free. The writer is thus an agent of change in disclosing the world as it is to his readers

NOT A "MILITANT" LITERATURE:

In 1964, the magazine *Clarté* hosted a debate on the question "What can literature do?," which Jean-Paul Sartre participated in. He tackled the question from the angle of committed literature as he had defined it in *What*

Is Literature?, but emphasized that committed literature is not the same as militant literature. It is committed because it seeks to provide the reader with an answer to the question of meaning. The reader seeks something that he lacks and, Sartre says, what he lacks is the meaning of life. The book's task is to give meaning to life. This meaning, however, is created by the free reader who encounters the signs on the page. ("Que peut la littérature? 107–27")

Having identified what writing does, Sartre asks himself, from the point of view of the writer, why one should write. There is an ethical requirement to be free and to make others free. We must add to that the role of human consciousness as we saw it in Chapter 1 and what Sartre refers to in the opening page of that section of the essay: consciousness unveils the world. It is consciousness that utters: "There is a world." At the same time, consciousness recognizes the utter contingency of its presence to being. One feels "inessential in relation to the thing revealed" (WL 23). Sartre continues and identifies why the writer feels the need to write: "One of the chief motives of artistic creation is certainly the need of feeling that we are essential in relationship to the world" (WL 24). This reminds us of Roquentin's decision to undertake to write a novel at the end of *Nausea*: feeling inessential and contingent, he thinks that creating something would be the way for his existence to be justified. For this to happen, though, there needs to be a dialogue between the writer and the reader. Sartre dismisses the idea that the writer writes for himself. To him, it is clear that writing entails reading, and that these acts necessitate two distinct agents. The writer unveils the world in his writing and needs a reader to validate the unveiling. It is only through the act of reading that the act of writing is justified and validated; as Roquentin had discovered, the writer is justified and essential in the consciousness of the reader, the same way the singer and composer of his favorite song are essential because Roquentin listens to their song. Thus, Sartre says:

All literary work is an appeal. To write is to make an appeal to the reader that he lead into objective existence the revelation which I have undertaken by means of language. […] the writer appeals to the reader's freedom to collaborate in the production of his work.

(WL 28–9)

In his ethics, Sartre concludes that we must make the Other free so that we may be free (see Chapter 6). Here, in the realm of literature, the writer must also appeal to the freedom of his reader. The appeal will be successful only if the reader's freedom is called upon. The writer must recognize the freedom of his reader and trust him. Sartre coins reading as a "pact of generosity" between writer and reader. This pact involves a party that discloses the world and another party that validates the disclosure. The disclosure is also an appeal to the reader to act in disclosing the world, since the disclosure will be brought to its end only by the act of reading. Thus the reader is as responsible for the work as the writer. Sartre says he is "compromised": "so both of us [writer and reader] bear the responsibility for the universe" (WL 39).

Sartre explains that the aesthetic imperative is grounded in the ethical imperative. Literature is about freedom, it involves the freedom of the writer and of the reader, it is a pact among them, and it can only be about freedom. This is true of all prose-writing, as he explains: "Whether he is an essayist, a pamphleteer, a satirist, or a novelist [he] has only one subject – freedom" (WL 41). And that is true regardless of the content of the work, whether it be individual or universal. This means, for Sartre, that the writer is thrown "into battle. Writing is a certain way of wanting freedom; once you have begun, you are engaged, willy-nilly" (WL 42). The writer is engaged in an ethical project but also, and by extension, in a political project. The writer unveils by naming certain things and this unveiling is already a change. The writer writes for a certain public: historically situated individuals. He too is an historically situated freedom. He unveils the world to the reader and this unveiling is an appeal for change. Indeed since, according to Sartre, the unveiling is a critical one:

Literature is, in essence, the subjectivity of a society in permanent revolution. […] the formal freedom of saying and the material freedom of doing complete each other, and that one should be used to demand the other […] its end is to appeal to the freedom of men so that they may realize and maintain the reign of human freedom.

(WL 107–8)

The writer thus has a key social and political role to play, as does every individual. His means of achieving his task will be through writing. That is why Sartre concludes his essay on literature by wishing that literature becomes ethical: it has a role to play ethically and politically. The writer is committed and commits his readers. They are tied to the project of freedom. That entails that the writer must retain the greatest degree of independence possible.

SARTRE AND THE NOBEL PRIZE

In mid-October 1964, Sartre read in the newspaper that the Swedish Academy was thinking of awarding him the Nobel Prize for Literature. He promptly wrote to the Academy, warning that he would refuse it. Ignoring his warning, the Academy awarded it to him "for his work which, rich in ideas and filled with the spirit of freedom and the quest for truth, has exerted a far-reaching influence on our age" (http://nobelprize.org/nobel_prizes/literature/laureates/1964/). Sartre found out on October 22, and immediately issued a text explaining why he refused the prize.

In this letter, which was read at the Academy the next day, and published in *Le Monde* on October 24, he explained that he had two sets of reasons to refuse the prize: personal reasons and objective reasons. His personal reasons were that he had always refused any type of distinction. As a writer, Sartre believed that, when writing, he was speaking and adopting political positions that were his own. If a distinction or award was tacked to his name, the reader would be confronted with a different type of position. The institution that awarded the prize would thus be committed to the position that the writer would adopt. In his letter published in *Le Monde*, Sartre said: "The writer must refuse to let himself be transformed into an institution" (my translation of "L'écrivain doit donc refuser de se laisser transformer en institution" [quoted in *Écrits* 403]). Among the objective reasons, Sartre mentioned the fact that the Nobel prizes seemed to be reserved for Western writers or rebellious writers from the then Eastern Bloc. Accepting the prize would mean that he would be letting himself be assimilated into these politics.

Sartre's refusal triggered much reaction. The most interesting one was André Breton, who declared that it was really a political act on Sartre's part in favor of the Eastern Bloc.

In order to speak freely and to appeal to other freedoms, the writer cannot appear to be speaking on behalf of certain institutions or party lines. That is problematic insofar as the writer must also commit himself beyond writing. That is a problem that strikes home for Sartre who, after the war, feels an urge to act in the world concretely. For Sartre himself, writing is a commitment, but one must also change the world. We will see in the next chapter how these ideas are articulated in political views and actions for Sartre.

SUMMARY

Sartre's war experience had a profound impact on him. It made him realize that he was a historical being and that he was engaged in the world. He decided that he had to be committed from then on. His somewhat unsuccessful attempt at playing a role in the Résistance led him to undertake another type of commitment: writing. In his presentation of *Les Temps modernes*, he first explained why he thought that writers are responsible for their writings and must commit themselves to bringing about change in the world. He refined these views in the essay *What Is Literature?* accounting for literature as the occasion for dialogue between the writer and the reader. The writer appeals to the freedom of his reader and, by unveiling the world, compromises him by making him feel responsible and committed to a world he now knows. The writer thus initiates change. Because writing is about freedom— even if only minimally in appealing to the reader's freedom—then writing is an ethical enterprise of making freedom flourish.

8

POLITICS

Sartre's committed literature may be understood as a way for him to fulfill the ethical goal that he had set for himself in the conclusion of *Being and Nothingness*. Even though he may have failed to successfully elaborate an ethical theory, it nevertheless remains that he considered the freedom of human beings to be the core value upon which ethics and politics should be grounded. His own commitment was an attempt to create favorable conditions for individual freedom to flourish. We have seen in the previous chapter that one such form of commitment was writing. Sartre considered that the writer could have an impact by unveiling the world to the reader through free dialogue, and making him responsible for it. The appeal to the reader is thus one way of promoting freedom. However, there was also another form of commitment for Sartre, one that is more direct and concrete: political action. Sartre examined many political movements and groups, and tried to position himself among them. In fact, for many people, Sartre was known only because of his political involvement and public standpoints.

In this chapter, we will examine Sartre's political stance. We will reexamine Sartre's discovery of historicity during the first months of the war, and how it led to his commitment. We will then look into Sartre's uneasy relations with the French Communist Party, or PCF. We will also examine how he undertook to revise Marxism, and how he proposed "Marxian existentialism" as a political "program" through the consideration of his *Search for a Method* and *Critique of Dialectical Reason*. Finally, we will consider some of Sartre's direct sociopolitical involvements.

HISTORICITY AND VIOLENCE: RECAP

As we have seen in the previous chapter, Sartre's experience as a soldier was the occasion that led to his discovery of his own historicity. But the war also unveiled the violent nature of history. Sartre's reflection on the war and his being-at-war entailed a reflection on the nature of violence and how individuals who are "caught up" in historical processes are affected by this violence. It is not only the violence of combat that he had in mind in these reflections. Rather, it is a somewhat ontological violence: the war is destructive of the world in a fundamental way. It tilts the world and realigns the meaning of all things and individuals within it. When war breaks out, all meanings are changed and the existence of all individuals is deeply affected. All beings become beings-at-war.

These reflections led Sartre to claim the necessity of commitment. Because one's being is affected by the state of the world (the example of war is blatant), it is important to act so that the world be one in which we can be free. War is destructive of the world and of freedom. One must act and choose in such a way that war be made impossible. For example, by choosing to participate in pacifist protests, one could have an impact in preventing wars. More generally, however, one must act and choose in order to create a world in which freedom can flourish. Literature is one type of activity that can promote freedom, but it might be necessary to complement it with more direct and immediate action, hence the necessity for Sartre to get involved. We discussed in the preceding chapter how Sartre came back to Paris in 1941 with this profound urge to act, and attempted to take part in the Résistance. We did not, however, examine how his newly found desire to commit himself politically was going to lead him in the political arena. This is what we turn to now.

SARTRE AND THE COMMUNIST PARTY

Once the war was over, the pathway for concrete political action for Sartre seemed to be involvement in a political party. Even though he felt some affinities with the French Communist Party (PCF), Sartre had never been interested in joining a political party. Unlike Paul Nizan and Raymond Aron, two close friends from the time he was attending the École Normale Supérieure (ENS), he did not feel any need to be formally involved in left-wing politics. At the time, Sartre read Marx but did not consider Marxist philosophy to be relevant.

KARL MARX (1818–83)

German philosopher Karl Marx has had a tremendous influence on the political reality of the twentieth century. His writings and analyses of capitalist society as one of exploitation have inspired many to launch Communist revolutions (most famously Lenin, who led Russia to the 1917 revolution that gave birth to the Soviet Union). Marx thought that, in a capitalist system, the worker and his labor are turned into commodities, and that the worker is alienated from the product of his labor. He suggested that the revolution of the proletariat would lead to the abolition of private property, and that a public ownership of means of production would eliminate alienation. The regime would ensue would be communism, where the following motto would be applied: "From each according to his ability; to each according to his need."

After his war experience, his attitude changed but he still did not join a party. David Drake explains: "Sartre had not voted in the elections and had no intention of applying to join the [French Communist] Party since his socialism was at odds with the centralized, hierarchical variant offered by the PCF" (Drake 26). In "On a raison de se révolter" (literally, "We are right to rebel," a discussion with Pierre Victor and Philippe Gavi published in 1974) Sartre explained that he considered himself an anti-hierarchical and libertarian socialist, who was in favor of direct democracy—not a good frame of mind to become a member of the PCF.

The PCF was an important player on the French political scene at the close of the war. It was a major party in the government led by de Gaulle, and had played a key role in the Résistance due to its mass support (it had earned 26.2 percent of votes in the October 1945 election). It took a firm stand against collaborators, and tried to consolidate its influence by introducing the members it had earned through the war to Marxism and the centralized democratic inner workings of the Party. While it sought to gain more support from intellectuals, it had been and continued to be suspicious of Sartre. During the war, the Party was even spreading rumours that Sartre had been released from the POW camp in order to garner and send information about the Résistance to the Germans. Sartre attended some meetings of the CNÉ (Comité National des Écrivains [National Committee of Writers], a committee that had connections with the PCF) and contributed some articles to the Communist-*résistant* journal, *Les Lettres françaises*. But all in all, his relationship with the PCF was a difficult one. Beauvoir explains: "On the political level, he felt that its sympathizers should play a role outside of the Communist party similar to that assumed inside other parties by the Opposition: a role that combined support and criticism." (FC 8). Sartre took this seriously, and criticized both the politics of the PCF and its ideological stance, specifically its particular understanding of Marxism. For its part, the PCF was critical of Sartre and existentialism, considering it to be yet another incarnation of bourgeois idealism. The PCF was also worried about the influence and attraction that existentialism had over the youth. Sartre humorously explained their behavior by saying: "It is very simple. At that time I had a clientele and they wanted to take it from me. That's all" (my translation of "C'est très simple, c'est qu'à ce moment-là j'avais de la clientèle, et qu'ils voulaient me reprendre ma clientèle. C'est tout" (*Sartre, un film* réalisé par A. Astruc & M. Contat, Gallimard, 1977, 83).

In 1948, relationships with the PCF worsened as Sartre joined the Rassemblement Démocratique Révolutionnaire (RDR). This group, launched by leftist non-communist journalists and intellectuals, wanted to draw support for a socialist type of democracy and positioned itself against the Stalinian type of governance. It thus stood in opposition to the PCF. The group published a journal, *La Gauche* ("The Left"), and held regular meetings. It was very popular at first, but its success waned rapidly. In the end, internal divisions and the lack of mass support marked the downfall of the group, from which Sartre resigned in October 1949.

In the early 1950s, Sartre drew closer to the PCF by getting involved in the Henri Martin affair. Henri Martin was a Communist sailor who had been imprisoned for distributing material against the war in Indochina (Vietnam; see Drake 83). Sartre had denounced US foreign policy publicly and repeatedly expressed his anti-colonialism previous to the affair. Because of that, the PCF saw him as a worthy ally. Following this, another affair infuriated Sartre and led him to lend his support: the Duclos affair. Jacques Duclos, an influential party member, had been arrested. The police had found two pigeons in his car that were allegedly used to communicate information to the Soviet Union. Sartre explained in an interview that it was such events that radicalized him and made him want to be a Communist fellow-traveler, as he liked to refer to himself. In 1952, he wrote and published the essay *The Communists and Peace*, which had the aim to clarify in what ways he agreed with the Communists, that is on very specific and limited issues. He was adamant: he was proceeding from his own philosophical principles, not from Marxism. About this, Drake comments that "Sartre may have moved to being a Communist fellow-traveler, but his frantically scribbled rebuttals of right-wing and far-left criticisms of the PCF came from a position of independence" (Drake 85–6).

Throughout his "fellow-traveling," Sartre was always cautious and maintained the distance he wanted from the PCF. He traveled to China, to the USSR, and grew more and more sympathetic toward the PCF, up until the Soviet invasion of Hungary in 1956. Sartre condemned the invasion, marking the end of his companionship with the PCF (who had endorsed the attack). However, the end of his involvement with the PCF did not mean the end of Sartre's involvement with Marxism.

SARTRE AND MARXISM

Sartre's hesitations about the PCF were accompanied by his reticence toward Marxism as a philosophy. We have seen in the preceding chapters that Sartre proposed a philosophy of freedom that posits the human individual as free and responsible for what he makes of himself. Marxism's deterministic views were precisely the stumbling block for Sartre's hesitation in this regard. William McBride explains:

> One of Sartre's greatest concerns throughout his career, obviously, has been to defend both the reality and (especially in his later writings) the future possibility of human freedom. It is this concern more than any other that explains

> his antipathy to the "orthodox" Marxist interpretation of materialism, which has traditionally been linked with a doctrine of flat and fairly rigid determinism. [...] Marx had no qualms about admitting that non-conscious entities can and do exert a direct influence over the activities of human consciousness. Sartre, on the other hand, with his Cartesian and Husserlian biases, has always resisted analyzing free human activity, or "internality," in "external," causal terms.
>
> (McBride 618–19)

Thus there seems to be an unbridgeable distance between Marxism and Sartre's existentialism: the former admits determinism while the latter rejects it. Obviously, this is of great impact with regards to any understanding of human action and responsibility, and it puts Sartre and Marxism at odds.

One of the problems facing Sartre's existentialism—at least as articulated in *Being and Nothingness*—comes in trying to account for the individual in a social context. It is one thing to say that the individual is situated, but it is another thing altogether to articulate that situation and theorize it. This was lacking in *Being and Nothingness*, and you will remember that the individual who emerged from it was conceived of as being in conflict with, and alienated by, the Other. Yet, as he was becoming more and more committed, Sartre felt a need to theorize the sociopolitical to better understand it and to better commit himself. His commitment was the direct result of his desire to be consistent with himself vis-à-vis freedom, but it required a theoretical foundation. This is why Sartre became increasingly interested in Marxist theory. An interesting question is whether this required him to abandon certain earlier positions—a question we will address after having examined Sartre's own argument for joining existentialism and Marxism.

THINKING THE SOCIAL SUBJECT: EXISTENTIALISM AND MARXISM

According to Sartrean scholar Thomas Flynn, the solution to the problems that emerge out of the ontological setting arises thanks to Sartre's appropriation of Marxism:

> As a Marxist, he [Sartre] believes that economics is decisive; but as an existentialist, he maintains the primacy of free, responsible praxis: one can always

make something of what others have made of him. The "others" have always constituted a problem for Sartre. In the mid '40s we saw them characterized as hellish. The success of a Sartrean social theory depends on his finding a more adequate solution to this question. In the *Critique* he approaches its resolution.

(Flynn 168)

It appears, then, that Sartre's position toward Marxism was always one of qualified approval. In an essay from 1946, entitled "Materialism and Revolution," he said:

In so far as it permits of coherent action, in so far as it expresses a concrete situation, in so far as millions of men find in it hope and the image of their conditions, materialism certainly must contain some truth. But that in no way means that it is wholly true as doctrine.

(*Literary and Philosophical Essays* 223)

As we have seen, Sartre was (and indeed, remained) critical of certain aspects of Marxism. In 1956, his position was clear:

For us, Marxism is not only a philosophy; it is the climate of our ideas, their feeding-ground, it is the true movement of what Hegel called the Objective Spirit. We see in it a cultural good of the left; better even: since the death of bourgeois thought, it is Culture by itself, since it is Marxism only that allows an understanding of men, works and events. Here is at least Marxism as it should be." (My translation of "Pour nous le marxisme n'est pas seulement une philosophie: c'est le climat de nos idées, le milieu où elles s'alimentent, c'est le mouvement vrai de ce que Hegel appelait l'Esprit Objectif. Nous voyons en lui un bien culturel de la gauche; mieux: depuis la mort de la pensée bourgeoise, il est à lui seul la Culture, car c'est lui seul qui permet de comprendre les hommes, les oeuvres et les événements. Voilà du moins le marxisme tel qu'il devrait être.)

("Le Réformisme et les fétiches" 110)

In *Search for a Method*, particularly the chapter "Marxism and Existentialism," Sartre clearly explains how the two "isms" come together. This is also the occasion for him to reflect on the place and function of philosophy.

According to Sartre, each epoch is under the seal of one dominant philosophy, which is that epoch's frame of reference. Marxism replaced

Hegelianism in the nineteenth century because it was in opposition to both Hegelianism and anti-Hegelian philosophies. Sartre thinks that periods of philosophical creation are rare. He identifies three that happened between the seventeenth and twentieth centuries: Descartes and Locke, Kant and Hegel, and Marx. According to Sartre, Marxism is "[…] the philosophy of our time. We cannot go beyond it because we have not gone beyond the circumstances which engendered it. Our thoughts, whatever they may be, can be formed only upon this humus; […]" (SM 30). A philosophy is located in time and in human culture, and is the expression of it. Moreover, Sartre says that it is a totalization of knowledge that entails a praxis: a philosophy proposes a way to understand the world and this understanding guides human action. One may thus adhere to a philosophy or be opposed to it. Either way, one makes of philosophy the fabric of one's life. To exemplify this, he examines the case of Søren Kierkegaard.

SØREN KIERKEGAARD (1813–55)

Kierkegaard is often regarded as the "father of existentialism." His philosophy focused on the concrete individual and subjective truth. This went against Hegelian philosophy, which was the trend of his day in Denmark. The main focus of his *Concluding Unscientific Postscript* (1846) is a criticism of rationalism and philosophical system-building as we find it in Hegel and other writers. To concentrate on the universal and absolute—as rationalist philosophers tend to do—is to miss the point of existence altogether. Kierkegaard thought that the rationalist philosopher is entirely mistaken in using reason and abstract thought to build a system of objective knowledge, when reality consists of those particular individual existences that deal with truth as subjective! Kierkegaard was thus in full disagreement with Hegel's worldview as the unfolding of Spirit through the history of the world, which he saw as reducing the role of the individual to its most minimal expression.

Taking position contra Hegel, Kierkegaard criticized the notion of objective knowledge and emphasized the importance of subjective knowledge, as well as the existence of the concrete individual over the universal objective subject. Kierkegaard's thinking emerges out of the soil of Hegel's philosophy. It is in reaction to Hegel, and thus cannot be conceived in this form without Hegel. Sartre will argue that the same can be said of the relationship between existentialism and Marxism. He says that existentialism is a "parasitical system" (SM 8).

Marxism is the thought of our time (well, at least of Sartre's time). Marx is concerned with:

> Concrete man whom he puts at the center of his research, that man who is defined simultaneously by his needs, by the material conditions of his existence, and by the nature of his world—that is, by his struggle against things and against men.
>
> (SM 14)

However, in its process of theorizing, Marxism tends to solidify in an ideology. When it does, it loses sight of the concrete individual. That is where existentialism kicks in. Sartre says:

> Marxism possesses theoretical bases, it embraces all human activity; but it no longer *knows* anything. Its concepts are *dictates*; its goal is no longer to increase what it knows but to be itself constituted a priori as an absolute Knowledge. In view of this twofold ignorance, existentialism has been able to return and to maintain itself because it reaffirmed the reality of men [...]
>
> (SM 28)

Existentialism does not stand in opposition to Marxism, however. It is a parasitic system and it stands more as a complement to Marxism than an opposition to it: "Existentialism and Marxism, on the contrary, aim at the same object; but Marxism has reabsorbed man into the idea, and existentialism seeks him everywhere *where he is* [...]" (SM 28). As long as Marxism dwells on ideas and constitutes itself as absolute knowledge, it will miss the existential concrete that it needs to also encompass. Existentialism is needed to complete the picture, as it considers the human being as more than a mere object of knowledge: the human being makes himself, his existence precedes its essence and, in that sense, it cannot be an object of knowledge. If we are to understand how the individual makes himself as a situated being, however, we need a philosophy that allows us to understand that situation. This is precisely what Marxism can do, since "it has been the most radical attempt to clarify the historical process in its totality" (SM 29), and it is the only philosophy, on Sartre's account, that "takes man in his totality – that is, in terms of the materiality of his condition" (SM 175). Providing the analysis of the situation, Marxism is needed to understand the concrete individual. It also needs existentialism, however, so as not to lose sight of that concrete individual. Sartre concludes that:

> From the day that Marxist thought will have taken on the human dimension (that is, the existential project) as the foundation of anthropological Knowledge, existentialism will no longer have any reason for being. Absorbed, surpassed and conserved by the totalizing movement of philosophy, it will cease to be a particular inquiry and will become the foundation of all inquiry.
>
> (SM 181)

Marxism and existentialism thus come together by positing human freedom as their central value. Marxism uncovers sources of alienation, and gives indications as to how to remedy that alienation. Existentialism also points out sources of alienation in the human individual, i.e. the temptation of bad faith. It requires that the individual make himself a free being. Juliette Simont underlines the fact: "If ethics exists for Sartre, it is an ethic of freedom and liberation" (Simont 179). Indeed, if we are to have an ethics of freedom, we must have free individuals, i.e. individuals freed from constraints, who will be able to mutually will one another's freedom. Marxism provides the tools needed to understand the material condition of individuals, and for us to think on how to improve it. In the same way that existentialism will wane when its particular analysis and understanding of human reality will no longer be needed by Marxism, Sartre explains that Marxism too will be superseded. It is the philosophy of our time, but not of all times: "As soon as there will exist *for everyone* a margin of *real* freedom beyond the production of life, Marxism will have lived out its span; a philosophy of freedom will take its place" (SM 34).

The work of the committed philosopher who produced circumstantial works answering to the exigencies of the political and historical context further carried Sartre on the Marxistic path. The *Critique of Dialectical Reason*, published in 1960, was written as an analysis of the for-itself as a historical being-in-the-world.

A WRITER UNDER PRESSURE

The *Critique of Dialectical Reason* was begun at the end of 1957 and was published in early 1960. Another mammoth work, at approximately 300,000 words, the *Critique* required of Sartre that he worked many hours a day. In her *Force of Circumstance*, Beauvoir recounts the conditions under which Sartre wrote. She depicts a climate of frenzy in which Sartre was

> working furiously at his *Critique de la Raison Dialectique*. It was not a case of writing as he ordinarily did, pausing to think and make corrections, tearing up a page, starting again; for hours at a stretch he raced across sheet after sheet without rereading them, as though absorbed by ideas that his pen, even at that speed, couldn't keep up with; to maintain this pace I could hear him crunching corydrane capsules, of which he managed to get through a tube a day.
>
> (FC 385)

Sartre had never been very careful with his health. A big consumer of whisky, wine, and corydrane (amphetamines), his consumption, allied with problems of hypertension, probably caused the loss of his eyesight.

In his commentary on the first volume of the *Critique*, Joseph Catalano suggests that one of the indirect objectives of this treatise was to point out the pitfalls that await socialism (Catalano 3). He also notes that Sartre had changed his mind concerning the bonds between his *Critique* and the work of Marx. While in *Search for a Method* Sartre was still uncertain about the links between his own thought and Marxism, he clarified the connection toward the end of his life, in an interview he gave for the Library of Living Philosophers' volume on his work, by declaring that the *Critique* was not Marxist (Catalano 5). As Drake has it:

> [The *Critique*] was the fruit of Sartre's reflections on Marxism. They had begun in the early 1950s when he was drawing close to the PCF. In the 1940s Sartre had contested Marxism from without (as in, for example, "Materialism and Revolution"). Now, however, his starting point, as he made clear in *Search for a Method* (published now as the first part of the *Critique*) was that Marxism was untranscendable; it was *the* philosophy of his time. One of the issues that

> Sartre was exploring was how to reconcile the dialectical method of (undog-
> matic) Marxism with existentialism.
>
> (Drake 107–8)

In the end, Sartre comes to utilize Marxism to complement his thinking on the for-itself. He needed to reflect on reciprocity, human interaction in a setting of scarcity and competition, and the possibility of common action. Marxism was the philosophy that could provide him with these theoretical tools. As Catalano puts it, the *Critique of Dialectical Reason* presents the historical and political dimensions that were missing from *Being and Nothingness* (see Catalano). In this sense, it was necessary that Sartre appropriated Marxism, even if it was in a rather non-orthodox iconoclastic fashion, but he is an existentialist who operates on Marxist grounds.

A "MARXIAN" EXISTENTIALISM?

Frederick Olafson suggests classifying Sartre's works in three periods: the first period is that of phenomenological psychology; the second period is that of the ontological inquiry into human existence (which is principally found in *Being and Nothingness*); the third period is that of the revision of Marxism, which begins with *Search for a Method* and peaks with the *Critique of Dialectical Reason* (see Olafson 287–93). Olafson remarks that the passage from the first to the second period does not make for a radical change, but is really an evolution, whereas the passage from the second to the third necessitates a revision—indeed a rejection—of Sartre's earlier views. According to him, Sartre would have to abandon his views on absolute freedom and the conflictual nature of interpersonal relationships in order to be able to explain, in Marxist terms, how the social and material conditions shape and mold the individual, and make political solidarity and socialism possible. Flynn has argued, on the contrary, that Sartre remains an existentialist throughout: the later writings present us with a Marxian existentialism that is continuous with earlier writings and their more individualistic considerations. He says: "Despite his talk of an existentialist 'ideology' adjective to Marxist 'knowledge' (savoir), *Sartre remains an existentialist*. Still, his existentialism should now be qualified as Marxian" (Flynn 172). What, then, does it borrow from Marxism?

McBride has pointed out that "the Marx whom Sartre often appears to find most attractive is Marx the historian [...]" (McBride 626). You will remember that, at the beginning of this chapter, we said that it was Sartre's discovery of historicity and violence that led him on the political path. No doubt Sartre's use of Marx is his own iconoclastic one. He does not end up a Marxist, but rather a philosopher who thinks through the social and political implications of his ontological positions on freedom, borrowing from Marxism the tools he needs. His theoretical political evolution may be explained in terms of an "[...] ontological ascent from consciousness to history, by way of the self, the other, and the group [...]" (Caws, *Sartre* 31). What Sartre needed, following the Second World War, was a way to think about action. In a 1975 interview, he explains:

> There is an evolution [in my thinking], but I don't think there is a break. The great change in my thinking was the war: 1939–40, the Occupation, the Resistance, the liberation of Paris. All that made me move beyond traditional philosophical thinking to thinking in which philosophy and action are connected, in which theory and practice are joined: the thought of Marx, of Kierkegaard, of Nietzsche, of philosophers who could be taken as a point of departure for understanding twentieth-century thought.
>
> (Interview 12)

COMMITTED TO FREEDOM

What Sartre was committed to throughout his life, and what he articulated his thought and action around, was the fundamental notion of freedom. He elaborated an existential philosophy about the free human being. He wrote novels, short stories, and plays on the problems that face the individual as a free and situated being. He wrote circumstantial essays to unveil the world, thus appealing to the freedom of his readers, and acting to change the world to make it more freedom-friendly. He theorized the sociopolitical reality of the individual by making use of Marxism in the later philosophical essays that we just discussed. He also acted to promote freedom, however, in becoming an activist and making concrete gestures. Using his notoriety, Sartre was part of many battles to foster freedom and create material conditions in which individuals could be free.

He protested against France's participation in the Algerian war (1954–62). *Les Temps modernes* had published articles on the situation in 1954 and, in 1955, Sartre publicly took a stand. He wrote essays, articles, gave public speeches, participated in marches, and signed petitions. He was opposed to the war because it was an attempt on France's part to maintain a colonialist regime that was against the liberation of the Algerian people. The motivation was to try to create a world in which freedom can flourish; freedom could not flourish in a subdued Algeria. Sartre had been reflecting on oppression and colonialism for a while, and his reflections once again were translated into concrete commitment on his part. The same motivation was at work when Sartre protested the Vietnam war: he refused to visit Cornell University in protest against the American involvement in the war, and accepted Bertrand Russell's invitation to be part of a tribunal. British philosopher Bertrand Russell (1872–1970) had published the essay *War Crimes in Vietnam* in 1966, and invited intellectuals to join him and form a tribunal that was going to investigate charges of war crimes on the part of the American government. The tribunal found the American government guilty of the charge, and also of genocide. Russell, who was then aged 94, could not attend deliberations, and Sartre presided the tribunal.

On a more local front, Sartre was also involved in the student revolts of May 1968. He was not an instigator, and was even taken by surprise by the uprising. However, he quickly contributed his support in an effort to understand what the French youth aspired to. Given that their movement was anti-bourgeois, leftist, and yet anti-Soviet, Sartre found natural allies in the movement. He lent his voice to support their claims, again with the advent of freedom as a motivation. His last political association was with the French Maoists. In 1970, he was invited to become the *directeur* of the Maoist newspaper *La Cause du Peuple* (The People's Cause). Wanting to defend freedom of expression, he agreed. He was not very familiar with the group's political positions at the time, but grew increasingly interested. He was attracted by their closeness to workers, their revolutionary attitude, and their desire for concrete action. The Maoists were ideologically closer to Sartre's libertarian socialism than the PCF had been or could ever be. His involvement with the Maoists was similar, too, in that he never officially joined the movement. Again, he wanted to work concretely and actively to foster liberation and freedom yet wanted also to retain his position of lucid critic, thus playing the role of the committed intellectual.

SUMMARY

Sartre's political involvement was to be a complement to his committed literature. While close to the socialist ideology of the PCF, Sartre's relations with it were tense and difficult. They drew closer together in the early 1950s, when Sartre became a "Communist fellow-traveler." They parted ways, however, following Sartre's harsh criticism of the Soviet invasion of Hungary in 1956. All the while, Sartre was thinking the political and offering an analysis of Marxism in hope to articulate it with existentialism. His *Search for a Method* was the outcome of this reflection. The *Critique of Dialectical Reason* presented Sartre's theorizing of the for-itself as a historical and social being that could act in a group, thus remedying a lack in Sartre's earlier philosophy, which tended to think of interpersonal relations in terms of conflict. Throughout his political commitment and theoretical writings with Marxist leanings, Sartre remained committed to freedom and the necessity to act in the world so as to make it flourish.

AFTER SARTRE

It is undeniable that Sartre, the "total intellectual," left a mark on the twentieth century. His writings, along with his manifold commitments to the social causes of his day, have been influential in shaping the way we understand the world and our place within it. His influence has been felt in many realms of culture: literature, theater, politics, and—most importantly—philosophy.

While he was considering Marxism through his existentialist perspective, Sartre claimed that Marxism was the "philosophy of our time." His argument was that each epoch was grounded in a philosophy, and that every writer and philosopher was writing in light of that philosophy—whether speaking in its terms or critiquing it. Can the same be argued of Sartre? Was he the "intellectual of our time" with whom all writers and philosophers were engaged in a dialogue, willy-nilly? The titles of both John Gerassi's 1989 biography, *Jean-Paul Sartre: Hated Conscience of his Century,* and Bernard-Henri Lévy's *Le Siècle de Sartre* (2000), convey the idea that Sartre was *the* thinker of the twentieth century—the one with or against whom one would think and write. As I have shown in this book, Sartre was active on the French intellectual scene from the 1930s until his death in 1980. While his philosophy certainly was a pole of attraction in the second half of the 1940s and early 1950s, the waning of existentialism also meant a displacement from the center of intellectual life to its margins for Sartre. He remained influential after this time, but in a different way.

In this concluding chapter, we will assess the importance of Sartre's existentialism and its impact on the philosophical movements that followed. We began our inquiry into Sartre's thinking by pointing out how much it departed from traditional rationalistic philosophy. His existentialism, articulated in literary and philosophical works, proposed a new way to understand the human subject in the world. This is also true of some other philosophical movements like structuralism, poststructuralism, and deconstruction. We will see how these philosophical movements are positioned vis-à-vis Sartre, and we will also see how some of the key thinkers of these movements owed some of their ideas to Sartre's influence. To begin, however, we will examine how the philosophy of *Being and Nothingness* has impacted the development of feminism via its possible influence on Sartre's closest contemporary, Simone de Beauvoir.

THE THORNY QUESTION OF INFLUENCE

In her writings, Beauvoir has often claimed that she was merely adopting the tenets of existentialism as expounded in Sartre's writings. Questioned about her own work and its relation to Sartre's, she has asserted that *he* was the philosopher, not her (in interviews with Margaret A. Simons for example). Questioned on whether she could have influenced him, she refused the claim: she was merely a writer; how could she have influenced him philosophically, if she was not doing philosophy? Her stance on the matter has been an annoyance to Beauvoir scholars. Immersed in her writings, they clearly see her philosophical originality and wish to demonstrate that her ideas, while intersecting with those of Sartre, were truly her own. The very recent publication of her student diaries (from 1926–7) show a young woman who is already developing her own existential reflections, well before her meeting with Sartre.

Some scholars have shown that Beauvoir's elaboration of certain ideas has been influential on Sartre's philosophical development. For example, in Chapter 3, we refered to how Sonia Kruks demonstrated the impact Beauvoir had on Sartre's notion of freedom (Kruks, "Teaching Sartre About Freedom"). The Beauvoir centenary in 2008 provided another occasion for scholars to assess the philosophical relationship between Beauvoir and Sartre, and to weigh the question of influence. It can be argued that, between the two, we find a criss-crossing of influence where both share and think with the other, and sometimes also against the other (see Daigle and Golomb [eds.], *Beauvoir and Sartre: The Riddle of Influence*).

In that sense, Sartre can be said to be the philosopher with whom and against whom Beauvoir thinks. It is with him that she thinks the notions of project and interpersonal relations in *Pyrrhus and Cinéas* (1944). But she goes beyond him in thinking about the ambiguity of such relations, and about the situation of the human being. Likewise, in *The Ethics of Ambiguity* from 1947, she also elaborates on the notion of freedom, detailing and refining it in a way that Sartre had not yet considered and would only consider in his writings of the 1950s (see Chapter 3). Acknowledging the weight of situation much more than Sartre was ready to at the time, Beauvoir distinguished between ontological freedom and moral freedom, a distinction that was going to, in its turn, influence Sartre (see Kruks). In her major work, *The Second Sex* (1949), Beauvoir grounded large parts of her analyses of what it means to be a woman on the existentialist notion of "existence precedes essence." Without naming Sartre, she says in her introduction that "our perspective is that of existentialist ethics" (*The Second Sex* xxxiv). It is because existence precedes essence that it is funda-mentally wrong to talk about such things as the eternal feminine or an essence of femininity that women should strive to embody. She remarks: "One is not born, but rather becomes, a woman." (*The Second Sex* 267). All human beings make themselves what they are. There is no destiny, and the female human being may choose to make herself a woman or not. Beauvoir thinks with Sartre that the individual makes him/herself and is fully responsible for what he/she makes of him/herself, but, as we will see, she thinks beyond him and against him regarding the body and sexuality.

We have seen in Chapter 5 that feminists have been very critical of Sartre's discussion of human sexuality, more specifically, that some regarded his views as being patriarchal and sexist. While Beauvoir does not engage in an open criticism of Sartre's views in general, it can be argued that the views she presents in *The Second Sex* are an implicit critical reappropriation of Sartre. Again, Beauvoir takes Sar-tre's philosophy as a springboard to go further than he did. While he did not discuss how the fact that consciousness is embodied makes a difference to how consciousness exists as sexual, Beauvoir makes it the core of her argument. She thus pushes Sartre's existentialist and phenomenological thought further in thinking about sex and gender. Beauvoir's work has become a foundational text of feminist and gender theory (the American poststructuralist feminist, Judith Butler, for example, has indicated how much Sartre's philosophy was influential for her). With this example, Sartre's influence is shown to be more far-reaching than it initially appears, and proves to be of significant use in philosophical approaches that, on the surface, seem foreign to it.

STRUCTURALISM AND POSTSTRUCTURALISM

While Sartre and other philosophers were leading the movement of existentialism, another movement was also flourishing at the same time. Structuralism, with such figures as Michel Foucault, Claude Lévi-Strauss (1908-), Jacques Lacan (1901–81), and Roland Barthes (1915–80). Existentialism and structuralism are generally seen as being in opposition; attacks and criticisms from both camps have reinforced this impression. However, some scholars have shown that there might be more that brings Sartre and the structuralists together than that separates them. In an essay titled "Sartrean Structuralism?," Peter Caws argues that "Sartre's refusal to be called a structuralist, like Foucault's, does not prevent the rest of us from enrolling him on the side of Structuralism" (Caws, "Sartrean Structuralism" 314). Caws thinks that there are fundamental points at which the reconciliation is impossible, but that both taken together can offer a view that is richer than what each can offer in isolation, namely an articulation of the theoretical and the existential.

Structuralism, as it is elaborated in the works of Lévi-Strauss and Foucault, for example, focuses on structures, on "meaningful wholes." It considers such things to be the structures of "language, kinship, political practice," and looks at how these structures are established and how they operate. However, while conducting the examination, its very focus leads the structuralist to move away from the human element. As Caws puts it:

> The upshot is a theory of the human world that dispenses with humans. It was this sort of thing that Sartre could not stomach; in one way or another all his

While Sartre wishes to acknowledge the role that structures play in the world, for him, the world is still one that is made by consciousness through its actions and interpretation.

A professor of mine, one of structuralist allegiance, once said of Sartre: "Sartre, pooh! That stinks of subjectivity!" With this utterance, he was summing up the divide between structuralism and existentialism. Indeed, Sartre and structuralists cannot agree on the role played by the acting individual, because the structuralist sees structures has having a life of their own, so to speak. For Sartre, structures exist insofar as there are humans in the world who make use of them. Human individuals are affected by these structures because they are situated consciousnesses. It is because the individual is situated that it even matters to understand structures in the first place. Structures are thus the fabric of the individual's situation. Understanding them allows one to better understand the individual. For Sartre, the two always go hand in hand. Caws concludes that "For Lévi-Strauss subjectivity and agency drop out in favor of an ontological objectivity of structure. For Sartre the elimination of the subject and the reification of the structure are equally unthinkable" (Caws, "Sartrean Structuralism" 308). While this statement is about Sartre and Lévi-Strauss specifically, it also extends to the positions held by other structuralists.

No matter how far structuralists want to go with the elimination of the subject (from a partial elimination to the death of the subject announced by Foucault, among others) it remains that Sartre's revision and rejection of the traditional notion of subjectivity was instrumental in making structuralism's radical rejection possible. In fact, as Christina Howells points out, Sartre himself declared man to be impossible in his *Critique of Dialectical Reason*. As she explains, Sartre had steadfastly rejected individual humanism in *Nausea,* and had posited the self as a worldly construct in the *Transcendence of the Ego* (Howells 327). As early as the 1930s, then, the ground was prepared for structuralism's radical positions on the subject. In Sartre, as we have said above, the subject always plays a role, however weak it might be, since " ... the subject may be deferred, dissolved, and deconstructed, but it is not relinquished" (Howells 342). In contrast to Sartre (and, I think, thanks to his preliminary work on decentering the ego in his early philosophy) the structuralists eliminate the subject altogether. Foucault and Derrida claim his death, Lacan decenters it radically, Deleuze and Guattari replace the "I" with "it," and push the iconoclastic critique to the point of replacing the "I think, I speak" with "it shits." (Howells 344).

While the latter may be shocking, it still bears some resemblance to the notion of pre-reflective consciousness expounded in *The Transcendence of the Ego*, wherein Sartre replaced the "I think therefore I am" with "There is consciousness, therefore I am." What then? Why do structuralists criticize Sartre so harshly and, apparently, misunderstand his positions on the subject, thinking that he clings to a traditional view? While some structuralists remained very critical of Sartre's philosophy, not all of them were in fact dismissive of it. Barthes, for example, dared recognize Sartre as the one great intellectual influence on his thought, along with Bertolt Brecht. He was an avid reader of Sartre's and commented on his work approvingly, despite the theoretical distance he felt from him. For example, he acclaimed Sartre's studies of Baudelaire and Genet for being existential psychoanalyses that involved examining the authors and not just their works. Barthes' own position on this, in a nutshell, is that the author should be absent from literary analyses.

Gilles Deleuze (1925–95) did not shy away from declaring Sartre to have been his master (see his interview for the journal *Arts* in November 1964). Deleuze saw in him a creator who successfully invented a new way of life—and a new way of philosophizing—after the war. He also appreciated how Sartre was able to extract from phenomenology the idea of immanence, i.e. the world that individuals live in. Jacques Lacan (1901–81) also recognized the influence of Sartre on his work in psychoanalytic theory. Specifically, he appreciated the analyses of the ego of *The Transcendence of the Ego* and *Being and Nothingness*. His positions on the formation of the ego, however, still remained different than those of Sartre—Lacan presenting it as the result of the inner workings of systems of language. Pierre Bourdieu (1930–2002), a major sociologist, and one who had been politically committed since the 1960s, recognized Sartre's notion of the committed intellectual as a key idea. He thought that this notion must be defended, and that intellectuals must be politically active in the way that Sartre had proposed. Theoretically, Bourdieu uses some notions of Sartre's phenomenology in order to resist the dehumanization of structuralism, a method that he puts to work in his analyses. Thus, with the help of Sartre, Bourdieu tries to keep the human within the structures.

While Michel Foucault and Sartre were philosophically at odds, they shared some political battles (both supported the student uprisings of May 1968, for example). Foucault, however, had been very critical of Sartre's philosophy. He remarked: "The *Critique of Dialectical Reason* is the magnificent and pathetic attempt of a nineteenth-century man to think the twentieth" (my translation of "La *Critique de la Raison Dialectique*, c'est le magnifique et pathétique effort d'un homme du XIXème siècle pour penser le XXème siècle" [Foucault, *Dits et écrits*, vol. 1, 541–2]). This is reminiscent of what his teacher, Louis Althusser, once said of Sartre's *Being and Nothingness* and *Critique of Dialectical Reason*: that they were a couple of long novels!) However, Foucault's later turn toward the care of the self shows that he shares Sartre's ethical concerns with authenticity. Foucault's and Sartre's notions of the self remain different, though: the former presents it as the product of structures, the latter presents the self as initiating them.

To round up our inquiry into this vein of influence, we must consider the relationship between Sartre and Jacques Derrida (1930–2004). Initially very critical of Sartre's philosophy, Derrida reproached him with humanism and a metaphysical attitude toward the subject. Taking part in the deconstructing and dissolution of the subject, Derrida could not accept Sartre's emphasis on individual consciousness. However, Derrida later attenuated his position and thought that rather than having been dissolved, the subject had been reinterpreted and resituated. It is important to the later Derrida to reevaluate our understanding of "subject" so as to understand that "it is naïve to speak of 'the Subject' as if it were a mythical entity that has now been abandoned" (Howells 349). Derrida's later position on the subject brought him closer to Sartre than he had been for many years, indeed since he was acquainted with Husserl, Heidegger, and Blanchot through reading Sartre.

OTHER HEIRS

It would be a mistake to think that Sartre's impact on the development of philosophy is reduced to structuralism and poststructuralism. Many other thinkers can be seen as influenced by his thought. French thinkers such as Alain Badiou, Jean-Luc Nancy, Michel Henry, André

Gorz, and Francis Jeanson, have all been influenced by one aspect or another of Sartre's mammoth enterprise in their rethinking of the human experience in the twentieth century. Interestingly, analytic philosophers of mind are growingly interested in Sartre's analyses of consciousness. Sartre's theoretical views on literature and theater continue to draw attention in literary studies, even if his own theatrical works have come to be classified as traditional.

What is intriguing in trying to assess the legacy of Sartre's philosophy is to note how much resistance there is to acknowledging Sartre as a predecessor. It almost seems, in certain cases, that the level to which Sartre has been dismissed makes it unfashionable to even claim him as an influence. Michel Rybalka talks about "Sartrophobia" in the intellectual spheres of France (*Dictionnaire Sartre* 36–7). Rybalka explains that to appreciate Sartre or not has often been a political gesture: appreciated by leftists, not so much by rightists. I think this "Sartrophobia," however, also extends to philosophers and scholars who have followed Sartre. Because the notion of the subject has fallen into disgrace during the wave of structuralism and poststructuralism, it is more fashionable to turn to Heidegger than to Sartre. Indeed, Heidegger's *Dasein* (his key term to designate the human being in the world) is supposedly impersonal. *Dasein* thus better suits a philosophy that claims to have left the subject behind than a Sartrean being for-itself that is a consciousness immersed in the world. It remains, however, that Sartre's reflections inform the new philosophers' analyses in many ways, prompting them to disagree, to go beyond him, or to think alongside him.

POLITICAL LEGACY

In his essay "The Sartre Centenary: Why Sartre Now?," William McBride argues that Sartre's legacy is philosophical but also—and importantly—political. Sartre's political stance has often been controversial, had drawn various reactions while he was alive, and continues to do so to this day. A special issue of the French magazine *L'Histoire* was asking the question "Was Sartre always wrong?" According to McBride, not only was Sartre *not* always wrong but he was so right that he can be helpful in thinking our political reality now.

Has the world changed much since Sartre's time? Probably the biggest change is that of the fall of the Eastern bloc at the end of the

1980s, and the fall of Communist regimes. However, that fall did not mean the fall of all oppressive regimes: the world is still inequitable both at national and international levels. Nationally, most countries suffer from class division and economic inequities. Internationally, the split between the "first world" and "other worlds" ("second," "third," and even "fourth") is greater than ever, and increasing at a rapid pace. McBride suggests that:

> The world is enmired in a situation of extreme malaise, in which the rich–poor gap is demonstrably greater than ever, the hypocrisy of the claim that elections and other political processes are achieving democratic outcomes is becoming more evident daily [...] The landscape is changing in such a way that Sartre's general rage against the fundamental injustices of contemporary society now again begins to seem more important than his occasional political mistakes—more important, and more justified.
>
> (McBride, 455–6)

If the world is still not one that fosters the flourishing of freedom for all individuals, and if its power dynamics are still the same, as McBride and many others would argue, then indeed Sartre's philosophy can be called upon to understand the world, but also to propose solutions.

SARTRE TODAY

The field of Sartre studies has been very active, as books and articles continue to appear and conferences on Sartre's works are held world-wide. You will find in the annotated bibliography information on specific works, but what I would like to discuss here are the themes that draw the attention of scholars.

There is a lot of current interest in Sartre's import to phenomenology. A good number of scholars are working on the early writings of the 1930s, and investigating how Sartre appropriated Husserl's phenomenology. Vincent de Coorebyter's new edition of *The Transcendence of the Ego* (2003) has given a new impetus to this line of inquiry. In relation to that, attention is also paid to how phenomenology is articulated with the existentialist position. This was not the case for Merleau-Ponty, who took a different, more epistemological path.

Scholars continue to be interested in the *Critique of Dialectical Reason* and other political texts in coming to understand notions of alienation, alterity, oppression, praxis, group action, but also—and more broadly—history itself. In that sense, Sartre has been brought in fruitful confrontation with Foucault, thanks to Thomas Flynn's *Sartre, Foucault, and Historical Reason* (1997). Other political writings of Sartre draw a lot of interest, notably the preface to Fanon's *The Wretched of the Earth* and *Anti-Semite and Jew*. While the former is being used in critical race theory and analyses of oppression, the latter has triggered interest in the connection between Sartre and Judaism (Jonathan Judaken's *Jean-Paul Sartre and 'the Jewish Question': Anti-anti-semitism and the Politics of the French Intellectual* (2006) has examined this problem). Another interesting theme is that of violence. Many studies have appeared on the question of violence in Sartre. It is both a political and an ethical question. As a proponent of freedom, Sartre was surprisingly supportive of violence when justified. This has puzzled interpreters who have tried to understand what is at work in Sartre's thought. The title of Ronald Santoni's book on the matter conveys that puzzlement well: *Sartre on Violence: Curiously Ambivalent.*

Ethical questions have always been of great interest for Sartrean scholars—for many reasons. As we suggested in earlier chapters, it is a fundamental question, and one that Sartre leaves somewhat unanswered. So many of his writings raise moral questions, and yet he never wrote the promised ethical treatise. Before the publication of the *Notebooks for an Ethics*, many studies tried to extract an ethics from the existent corpus of works. Since its posthumous publication in 1983, a lot of work has been done in analyzing the *Notebooks*. For one, scholars have explained how the notion of authenticity and conversion to the Other that we find elaborated in its pages can be articulated with the views previously exposed in *Being and Nothingness* and other published texts. Authenticity remains a central theme of inquiry in Sartrean scholarship.

Sartre's relevance today does not only pertain to his philosophical and political output. His literature and theater continue to be the focus of attention as well. *Nausea* is investigated from the literary and philosophical front alike. *The Roads to Freedom* trilogy and its wealth of styles is a perfect playground for literary theorists. The publication of the Gallimard Pléiade edition of Sartre's *Théâtre Complet* (2005) and the many other publications of studies on Sartre's theater are indicative of the liveliness of the interest for this part of his work. Sartre's literary theory, as elaborated in *What Is Literature?* and other literary essays, also continues to attract interest.

Sartre's relation, philosophical or otherwise, with contemporary thinkers is a favored topic too. Sartre did not acknowledge a wealth of influences on his thought, and yet a close examination of his works shows that many past philosophers and writers have played a role in the formation of his thought. Likewise, and as I have discussed earlier in this chapter, the number of thinkers that stand to have been influenced by Sartre, and the variety of fields in which they are to be found, is an indication that we must expect more studies to appear.

This is but a short survey of all the activity that surrounds Sartre's works today. Existentialism may no longer be a buzzword, but the central themes that it addresses are so fundamental to human experience that they remain of actuality at all times. For this reason, I suspect that Sartre's works will always be of interest, because they tackle problems from the lived experience of the individual, something that is unfortunately often missing in contemporary philosophical approaches. Because human beings always seek to make sense of their experience, a philosophy that places it at its center—the way Sartre's does—is bound to be of continued interest.

FURTHER READING

WORKS BY SARTRE

While working your way through this book, you will have noticed that Sartre was indeed a prolific writer. Here, I list all of the major works he published, but avoid listing all the individual articles he published, his minor plays, and the interviews he gave, for the list would be far too expansive to include here. Each work is listed in the chronological order of its original (French) publication date. The titles of some plays are accompanied by two dates: this is an indication that the play premiered in a different year than that when it was published. In these cases, the first date is that of the premiere and the second that of the publication.

The Imagination (*L'Imagination*, Paris, Alcan, 1936)
This essay was the introduction to a larger study on the faculty of imagination. The larger study appeared four years later after Sartre had reworked it as *L'Imaginaire*. In this piece, he examines a few traditional conceptions of imagination and contrasts them with Husserl's.

The Transcendence of the Ego (*La Transcendance de l'Ego*, initially published in *Recherches philosophiques*, no. 6, 1936–7, pp. 85–123; published as a book by Vrin in 1965, edited and annotated by Sylvie Le Bon)
This essay is crucial in understanding Sartre's contribution to the phenomenological tradition. In it, he sets out the foundation of his

existentialist philosophy of the free consciousness to be found in the later *Being and Nothingness*. I recommend the French edition, *La Transcendance de l'Ego et autres textes phénoménologiques*. Textes introduits et annotés par Vincent de Coorebyter. Vrin, 2003. This edition of Sartre's key phenomenological essay is extremely helpful in contrasting the essay with other, shorter, essays on Husserl's phenomenology. The introduction written by de Coorebyter is excellent and sheds important light on Sartre's approach to phenomenology. It details the philosophical path taken by Sartre through the years and how his position vis-à-vis Husserl evolved accordingly.

Nausea (La Nausée, Paris, Gallimard, 1938)
Sartre's first published novel and a must-read for anybody interested in Sartre's existentialist philosophy. As we have seen, it tackles many of the themes to be found in his most important philosophical writings, such as *Transcendence of the Ego* and *Being and Nothingness*. Some readers find it to be a rather odd novel because of its structure (as the supposed publication of the protagonist, Antoine Roquentin's, diary) but it is well worth the effort to read.

The Wall (Le Mur, Paris, Gallimard, 1939)
This is the only collection of short stories that Sartre published. It contains five short stories, all inquiring into the lives of characters that are all flawed in a certain way. The book was deemed a success immediately after its publication. The collection is extremely interesting to read with the notions of bad faith and authenticity in mind.

A Sketch for a Theory of the Emotions (Esquisse d'une théorie des émotions, Paris, Hermann, 1939)
This essay explores the relationship between consciousness and its emotions and the world. Thus the essay goes beyond an understanding of consciousness as a merely cognitive function. Contat and Rybalka deem it to be the best introduction to *Being and Nothingness*.

The Imaginary (L'Imaginaire, Paris, Gallimard, 1940)
This study is the reworked second part of *The Imagination* published in 1936. In it, Sartre examines such things as images and their perception as well as the capacity consciousness has to nihilate such images in order to create its own.

The Flies (Les Mouches, Paris, Gallimard, 1943)

This first published play marked Sartre's opportunity to put his ideas about freedom on stage. Under the garb of a classical tragedy, the play allowed for Sartre to speak about freedom in occupied Paris. Sartre had been able to fool the German censorship using such a strategy.

Being and Nothingness (*L'Être et le néant*, Paris, Gallimard, 1943)

Sartre's existentialist *magnum opus*. Subtitled "a phenomenological essay on ontology," this book presents an exploration of the lived reality of human consciousness. Through the use of the phenomenological method, it explores every aspect of the life of individual consciousness while polishing concepts already introduced in earlier publications. This work is the key to Sartre's existentialist-phenomenological philosophy.

No Exit (*Huis clos*, 1944; Paris, Gallimard, 1945)

This play presents the audience with three characters interacting and quarreling with each other in a rather unusual version of "hell": a single room with no windows and no way out. The play is known for putting the notions of being for-others and "the look" on stage and demonstrating, accordingly, the conflictual nature of interpersonal relations that Sartre had delineated in *Being and Nothingness*.

The Age of Reason (*L'Âge de raison*, 1945). First volume of the trilogy *The Roads of Freedom*.

This novel is written in a more conventional style than *Nausea*. Its main character, Mathieu, tries to live his life as an absolutely free individual, even when faced with various demands requiring that he bears responsibility for his deeds.

The Reprieve (*Le Sursis*, 1945). Second volume of the trilogy *The Roads of Freedom*

In this second installment, Sartre explores a different literary technique. The whole novel is an account of how many different characters experience a political crisis that precedes Word War II and spans over only a few days. The reader is taken from one character to the other sometimes in the middle of a sentence. Mathieu and other characters of the first volume of the trilogy evolve through these events but we are also acquainted with a myriad of others.

Existentialism is a Humanism (*L'Existentialisme est un humanisme*, Paris, Nagel, 1946)

A slightly modified transcript of a speech delivered by Sartre at Le Club Maintenant. Its aim was to popularize certain notions that had been discussed in *Being and Nothingness* for the general public while also dispelling certain myths attached to the then-growing movement of existentialism. The short booklet has been regarded as the most accessible of Sartre's works but Sartre sometimes regretted its publication as he thought that readers would be satisfied with it and not read his other, more complex, works.

Men Without Shadows (*Morts sans sépulture*, Lausanne, Marguerat, 1946)
This play explores the question of torture and responsibility. In it some résistance fighters are made prisoners and are questioned by their jailors who seek information about the resistance and one of its leaders.

The Respectful Prostitute (*La Putain respectueuse*, Paris, Nagel, 1946)
This play explores notions of authenticity and bad faith as well as moral responsibility. The main character, the prostitute Lizzie, is pressured to provide testimony that a black man is responsible for a crime that was in fact perpetrated by a white man. She is torn between telling the truth and giving in to the pressures.

Anti-Semite and Jew (*Réflexions sur la question juive*, Paris, Paul Morihien, 1946 [Gallimard: 1954])
In this essay, Sartre explores the questions of authenticity and bad faith as they relate to the problem of anti-Semitism. Sartre presents a damning portrait of anti-Semitism, thus proposing a stance that is anti-anti-Semitic.

Baudelaire (Paris, Gallimard, 1947)
This essay was initially written in order to serve as an introduction to an edition of Baudelaire's intimate writings (*écrits intimes*). Sartre focused on the character of Baudelaire, rather than on his poems. Thus, the essay can be seen to be in line with the existential psychoanalyses of Jean Genet (*Saint Genet comédien et martyr*) and Gustave Flaubert (*L'Idiot de la famille*). Here, Sartre explores the notion of the original choice of oneself.

The Chips are Down (*Les Jeux sont faits*, Paris, Nagel, 1947)
This is a script for a film that was put on screen by Jean Delannoy in 1947. It is one of many scripts that Sartre wrote. The two main characters are dead and wandering as ghosts. They meet and are given a chance to go back to life as they were predestined to be soul-mates but some mistake had prevented it from happening. They are given 24 hours to fall in love and accomplish their destiny. However, this is made difficult as each is distracted by their past lives.

Dirty Hands (Les Mains sales, 1948)
This play presents us with a political drama. The play was controversial in how it portrayed the Communists and Sartre had to later explain what he wanted to achieve with the play. Hugo, a young man of bourgeois origins, becomes the secretary of Hoederer, a leader of the Communist Party. His mission is to kill him because he is perceived as colluding with the bourgeoisie. Hugo hesitates as he grows to like Hoederer and finds accomplishing his mission difficult.

Iron in the Soul (La Mort dans l'âme, Paris, Gallimard, 1949). Third volume of the trilogy *The Roads of Freedom*
This volume returns to a more classical novelistic style. The first part revolves around Mathieu, who is a soldier engaged in the war and who has decided to put his freedom to work for others while the second part revolves around Brunet, who has been made a prisoner of war and seeks to advance what he perceives to be the Communist Party's agenda. While doing so, he struggles with his past decision to always obey the Party line, questioning himself about his own freedom.

The Devil and the Good Lord (Le Diable et le bon Dieu, Paris, Gallimard, 1951)
This play toys with the notions of belief, atheism, moral responsibility and values. The main character is shown to evolve through various stages and seeks to attain liberation through the realization that God does not exist and that he is the sole creator of values.

Saint Genet, Actor and Martyr (Saint Genet, comédien et martyr, Paris, Gallimard, 1952)
This is a book that Sartre wrote as the introduction to the complete works of the writer Jean Genet and is the first volume in this collection. This great piece is more than an introduction to Genet. In it, Sartre revisits some of the principles of his existential psychoanalysis presented in *Being and Nothingness* and gives them a new twist by combining them with a Marxist analysis.

Search for a Method (Questions de méthode, in Les Temps modernes, nos. 139 and 140, 1957; as the first section of Critique of Dialectical Reason, Paris, Gallimard, 1960 and as a single book in 1967)
In this essay, Sartre explains how existentialism and Marxism are compatible and why it is crucial to use the Marxist method of analysis. At the same time, he argues that it is important to remain critical of certain incarnations of that method.

The Condemned of Altona (Les Séquestrés d'Altona, 1959, Paris, Gallimard, 1960)

A theatrical exploration of the notion of moral responsibility and situated freedom. Frantz von Guerlach lives in a self-imposed sequestration that impacts his family. He testifies before a tribunal of crabs, the inhabitants of the thirtieth century, before whom he seeks to justify himself.

Critique of Dialectical Reason (Critique de la raison dialectique, précédé de *Questions de méthode*, Paris, Gallimard, 1960)

This major work is the analysis of the experience of the historical individual in a group. No longer thought of in isolation as in Sartre's previous works, the for-itself is here conceived as a political and social being that acts and interacts within social structures and pressures. This work constitutes a major shift from existentialism, even if it can be conceived as constituting its natural continuation.

Words (Les Mots, Paris, Gallimard, 1964)

Sartre's autobiography was a long-term endeavor. The final product of his years of work was this wonderful piece in which he wittingly revisits his early years. He reinterprets his childhood according to two defining themes: reading and writing. This autobiography can also be read in light of Sartre's existential psychoanalysis. Only, this time, he is the object of inquiry.

The Family Idiot (L'Idiot de la famille, Paris, Gallimard, first two volumes in 1971, third volume in 1972)

This monumental work remains incomplete. Sartre's blindness prevented him from completing his project. The family idiot is 19th-century novelist Gustave Flaubert whose works Sartre encountered at a young age. Fascinated by Flaubert, Sartre set out to conduct an inquiry into what made Flaubert Flaubert.

Situations I to *X*:

Published between 1947 and 1976 by Gallimard, the volumes titled *Situations* are collections of essays of various length and importance in the Sartrean corpus. Some are very specific to political issues and realities of their time while others pertain to more atemporal topics such as the question of the nature of literature (addressed in the 1947 *What is Literature?*, published as *Situations II*). Very important essays on politics are to be found in those volumes. However, it is sometimes difficult to locate these essays in English as they have not been systematically translated and the content of the editions that exist does not precisely match any of the volumes of the *Situations* series.

POSTHUMOUS PUBLICATIONS

In addition to all of his published material, some of the material Sartre had refrained from publishing (for various reasons) was published after his death. Some manuscripts are still unavailable to the public and await publication. The most important posthumous writings are as follows:

War Diaries (*Carnets de la drôle de guerre*, Paris, Gallimard; the 1983 edition contains five notebooks and is the basis for the English translation currently available. The 1995 edition contains one added notebook, the first, and is not available in English yet)

These notebooks constitute Sartre's diary while drafted as a soldier from September 1939 to his captivity in 1940. In them, Sartre gives an account of his daily life but also talks about his readings and philosophizes on important themes. Many pages of the notebooks are genuine drafts for *Being and Nothingness*.

Notebooks for an Ethics (*Cahiers pour une morale*, Paris, Gallimard, 1983)

Written between 1947 and 1948, these notebooks constitute an attempt on Sartre's part to work out an ethics on the basis of *Being and Nothingness* while providing a solution to the problem of authenticity. Sartre abandoned the project after having filled 10 notebooks. Two have been published in this edition while the others have not yet been found. They may even have been destroyed.

Truth and Existence (*Vérité et existence,* Paris, Gallimard, 1989)

This essay was written after the *Notebooks for an Ethics*. It explores the question of truth and the role that it plays for consciousness caught in the realm of intersubjectivity. Arlette Elkaïm-Sartre, responsible for the publication of the text, speculates that Sartre's reception of Heidegger's essay, "On the Essence of Truth," in 1948 might have triggered his desire to clarify the notion of truth for himself.

Critique of Dialectical Reason, volume 2 (*Critique de la raison dialectique*, vol. 2, Paris, Gallimard, 1985)

This second volume of the *Critique* explores the question of history and its intelligibility. It constitutes an important addition to the first volume that explores the individual in social settings.

Lettres au Castor et à quelques autres, volume 1: 1926–39 and volume 2: 1940–63
(Paris, Gallimard, 1983)

Volumes 1 and 2 were translated respectively as *Witness to my Life: The Letters of Jean-Paul Sartre to Simone de Beauvoir* and *Quiet Moments in a War: The Letters of Jean-Paul Sartre to Simone de Beauvoir*. The letters were published by Simone de Beauvoir after Sartre's death. Along with Beauvoir's letters to Sartre (which were published after her death), they constitute an invaluable resource toward attaining a comprehensive understanding of these two intellectuals' multifaceted lives.

SECONDARY LITERATURE ON SARTRE

Perry Anderson, Ronald Fraser, Quintin Hoare, and Simone de Beauvoir.
(2006) *Conversations with Jean-Paul Sartre*. London: Seagull Books

This is a collection of three interviews that Sartre gave. Two of those, "Itinerary of a Thought" and "Imperialist Morality," were published in the *New Left Review* in 1969 and 1967 respectively. The interview conducted by Simone de Beauvoir, "Simone de Beauvoir Questions Jean-Paul Sartre," appeared in *L'Arc* in 1975. These interviews present a mature Sartre who discusses various aspects of his thought and itinerary as well as on the political situation in the world. It is in the 1969 interview that Sartre famously disavows his early position on absolute freedom by saying: "It's incredible, I actually believed that!" (p. 5).

Thomas C. Anderson (1979) *The Foundation and Structure of Sartrean Ethics.*
Lawrence: The Regents Press of Kansas

This is the first of two books by Anderson that seeks to determine what a Sartrean ethics would be. In this first book, Anderson considers *Being and Nothingness* and the *Notebooks for an Ethics*. In addition, he turns to Beauvoir's *Ethics of Ambiguity* as the expression of the ethics that unfolds from *Being and Nothingness*.

Thomas C. Anderson. *Sartre's Two Ethics. From Authenticity to Integral Humanity.*
Chicago and LaSalle: Open Court, 1993

Anderson's second book on Sartrean ethics now takes into consideration Sartre's writings of the 1950s. Thus, Anderson examines the evolution in Sartre's thought from a philosophy that focuses on the individual in the 1940s to the opening to the Other that the Rome lecture and the notes for Cornell represent.

Ronald Aronson (2004) *Camus & Sartre. The Story of a Friendship and the Quarrel that Ended it*. Chicago and London: The University of Chicago Press
In this book, Aronson examines the Camus–Sartre relationship from the moment of their first encounter to the break between the two and beyond. Aronson shows that this relationship was complex and that the break that ended it was philosophically as well as politically motivated. His book combines biography with the history of philosophy.

Ronald Aronson (1987) *Sartre's Second Critique*. Chicago and London: The University of Chicago Press
In this book, Aronson offers a guide and commentary to the second volume of the *Critique of Dialectical Reason*. The manuscript was unavailable up until 1985 when it was published in French. It was translated into English in 2006. Aronson's commentary remains authoritative as it provides more than a mere account of the content but actually explains it. Given the difficulties of Sartre's text, the commentary is a must for anybody interested in it.

Ronald Aronson and Adrian van den Hoven (eds.) (1991) *Sartre Alive*. Detroit: Wayne State University Press
This important collection of essays gathers scholarly articles that investigate various aspects of Sartre's philosophy. One of these important contributions is that of Robert Stone and Elizabeth Bowman who discuss the unpublished lecture notes that Sartre had prepared for a conference at Cornell University but cancelled in protest against US intervention in Vietnam. It also contains an interview with Sartre conducted by Pierre Verstraeten, an important Sartre scholar.

Simone de Beauvoir's autobiographies (in chronological order): *Memoirs of a Dutiful Daughter, The Prime of Life, Force of Circumstance, All Said and Done, Adieux: A Farewell to Sartre* (in the same order with original publication date: *Mémoires d'une jeune fille rangée* (1958), *La Force de l'âge* (1960), *La Force des choses* (1963), *Tout compte fait* (1972), *La Cérémonie des adieux* suivi de *Entretiens avec Jean-Paul Sartre*, août–septembre 1974 (1981).
These five books tell the story of the couple's life from Beauvoir's perspective. The first book focuses on Beauvoir's childhood and youth but tells the story of the encounter with Sartre at the end of the volume. Thereupon, he becomes a central character in the remaining autobiographies. The last book of the series is a poignant narrative about

Sartre's last years, days, and moments, Beauvoir not shying away from describing the slow but certain decrepitude of her partner.

Linda A. Bell (1989) *Sartre's Ethics of Authenticity*. Tuscaloosa: University of Alabama Press
Contra many critics who assert that a Sartrean ethics is problematic or just plain impossible, Bell argues that focusing on the notions of authenticity and play allows one to uncover a viable ethics in Sartre.

Jean-Pierre Boulé (2005) *Sartre, Self-Formation and Masculinities*. New York and Oxford: Berghahn Books
Boulé's study brings to fruition a psycho-social analysis of Sartre's becoming in terms of his own gender. Boulé examines Sartre's life in view of his writings and vice versa, focusing on the impact childhood experiences and gender orientation had in his development.

Robert Bernasconi (2006) *How to Read Sartre*. London: Granta Books
This is an introductory book that focuses on key themes and notions in Sartre's philosophy such as the Other, contingency, bad faith, freedom, authenticity, and violence.

Joseph S. Catalano (1980) *A Commentary on Jean-Paul Sartre's* Being and Nothingness. University of Chicago Press. And Joseph S. Catalano (1986) *A Commentary on Jean-Paul Sartre's* Critique of Dialectical Reason, *volume 1, Theory of Practical Ensembles*. The University of Chicago Press
Catalano's commentaries assist the reader in tackling the two most difficult texts of the Sartrean corpus. They provide an introduction to the text under study and proceed to clarify and explain the theory exposed in each work. Catalano's explanations will be helpful to the inexperienced reader but also to the scholar who might find the text's theoretical intricacies complex.

Joseph Catalano (1996) *Good Faith and Other Essays: Perspectives on a Sartrean Ethics*. Lanham: Rowman and Littlefield
Dealing with both the early and the later Sartre, in this book Catalano explores the ethical connotations of notions such as the look, the third, and the group-in-fusion. He offers a Sartrean perspective on authenticity while examining weak and strong notions of good and bad faith.

Peter Caws (1979) *Sartre*. London: Routledge
Caws' book on Sartre is a scholarly examination of various aspects of his philosophy. It tackles such questions as the nature of consciousness,

the for-itself in relation to others, freedom, politics, and the problems of morality. A comprehensive study.

Annie Cohen-Solal. *Jean-Paul Sartre: A Life.* New York: New Press, 2005
(translation of Annie Cohen-Solal, *Sartre. 1905–90*, Paris: Gallimard, 1985)
This biography is the most exhaustive there is. Other authors have tackled some aspects of Sartre's life but this book does much more. With 960 pages in the French original, it aims to bring to life Sartre's whole existence in all its details. It combines the personal with the intellectual biography in a masterful way—and succeeds. A must for anybody interested in Sartre's life and how his ideas emerged.

Michel Contat and Michel Rybalka (1973) *The Writings of Jean-Paul Sartre.*
Evanston (IL): Northwestern University Press
This is the translation of *Les Écrits de Sartre: Chronologie, bibliographie commentée* published in 1970 by Gallimard. This mammoth work gives a detailed annotated bibliography of everything that Sartre has written, published, and discussed in interviews. It also gives dates of theater premieres as well as details of various editions of books. The work also contains some 32 texts that have been unearthed and are published for the first time. It also provides the user with three indexes (titles, journals, and names). It is an essential tool for Sartrean research. This bibliography has been supplemented by its authors with a bibliography of primary and secondary sources in their *Sartre: Bibliography. 1980–1992* (CNRS 1993).

Gary Cox (2008) *The Sartre Dictionary.* London: Continuum
This book is organized as a dictionary with entries for terms, concepts, works, and people that are relevant to Sartre studies.

Wilfrid Desan (1965) *The Marxism of Jean-Paul Sartre.* New York: Doubleday
Desan's book seeks to clarify whether Sartre can be said to have offered a Marxist philosophy and, if so, what type of Marxism we are faced with. Its object of analysis is the *Critique of Dialectical Reason* with some attention paid to other political writings, such as *Search for a Method.*

David Detmer (2008) *Sartre Explained. From Bad Faith to Authenticity.* Chicago and LaSalle: Open Court
This introductory book adopts an interesting approach. Spanning Sartre's whole writings, each chapter focuses on a single book, paying

equal attention to philosophical and literary works. A concluding chapter weaves threads together by discussing key Sartrean concepts.

David Drake (2005) *Sartre*. London: Haus Publishing
This introduction to Sartre focuses on Sartre as a political writer and activist. Drake traces the evolution of Sartre along these lines and focuses on his various commitments.

John Gerassi (1989) *Jean-Paul Sartre: Hated Conscience of his Century*. Chicago and London: The University of Chicago Press
This is the "official" biography of Sartre. Gerassi interviewed Sartre between 1974 and 1979 and had access to his papers. He also interviewed friends and foes of Sartre. Through this research, he writes the story of the making of this great intellectual.

Ronald Hayman (1986) *Writing Against: A Biography of Sartre*. London: Weidenfeld and Nicolson
The first major account of Sartre's life published in the English language. Although not nearly as comprehensive as that of Cohen-Solal in describing the personal details of Sartre's life, Hayman's biography is notable for carefully explaining the context and meaning of each of Sartre's major works. Additional emphasis is placed on showing how developments in Sartre's philosophical thinking are reflected through his political activism.

Christina Howells (ed.) (1992) *The Cambridge Companion to Sartre*. Cambridge: Cambridge University Press
In this collection of essays, scholars tackle some of the most important problems in Sartre's philosophy, from the early period focused on existential phenomenology to the later political developments of Sartre's thought. In addition, an appendix on the Hegel–Sartre connection sheds an important light on the supposed Hegelianism of *Being and Nothingness*.

Francis Jeanson (1980) *Sartre and the Problem of Morality*. Bloomington: Indiana University Press (translation of *Le Problème moral et la pensée de Sartre* (suivi *D'Un quidam nommé Sartre*). Lettre-préface de Jean-Paul Sartre. Paris: Seuil, 1965)
In this impressive study, Jeanson carefully examines the problem of morality as it unfolds in the existentialist writings of Sartre (such as *Nausea* and *Being and Nothingness*). In his preface to the work, Sartre

praised Jeanson for having been able to embrace and explicate his ethical thinking and for having been able to push it where he had not.

R. D. Laing and D. G. Cooper (1964) *Reason and Violence. A Decade of Sartre's Philosophy 1950–1960.* New York: Pantheon Books

This book is an introduction to the later Sartre's philosophy. Thus it focuses on such writings as *Saint Genet*, *Search for a Method* and the *Critique of Dialectical Reason* and illuminates Sartre's political transformation.

F. H. Lapointe and C. Lapointe (1981). *Jean-Paul Sartre and his Critics. An International Bibliography (1938–80).* Bowling Green (Ohio): Philosophy Documentation Center, Bowling Green State University

This is a good research tool as it gathers together all important writings published on Sartre between 1938 and 1980. For publications after 1980, one should consult Contat and Rybalka as well as *Sartre Studies International.*

Bernard-Henri Lévy (2003) *Sartre: The Philosopher of the Twentieth Century.* Cambridge: Polity Press. Translation of *Le Siècle de Sartre* published by Grasset in 2000

BHL's book is subtitled "Philosophical Investigation." In this ambitious work, he explores the many philosophical likes and dislikes of Sartre as well as the way his career unfolded through his various political stances. Lévy is successful in showing that Sartre was a "total" intellectual who had a tremendous impact on his century.

Thomas Martin (2002) *Oppression and the Human Condition. An Introduction to Sartrean Existentialism.* Lanham: Rowman & Littlefield

This is an introduction to the early Sartre via the specific angle of oppression. It answers two questions: what does the early Sartre have to say about oppression and to what use can we put these views? Martin presents us the case of anti-Semitic racism and sexism to show that Sartre's philosophy can help us understand and combat such instances of oppression as well as others.

Katherine J. Morris (2008) *Sartre.* Oxford: Blackwell

This introduction to Sartre's philosophy focuses on Sartre as phenomenologist of the life-world and the body. It thus pays a great deal of attention to the early writings as well as Sartre's methodology or, in Morris' words, what Sartre is in fact doing with philosophy. She proposes to understand him as proposing a therapy to cure intellectual prejudices.

Julien S. Murphy (ed.) (1999) *Feminist Interpretations of Jean-Paul Sartre*. University Park (PA): Pennsylvania State University Press

This collection of essays appears in the collection "Re-reading the canon" that seeks to offer a feminist perspective on key thinkers. Here, Sartre's thought is scrutinized by scholars to uncover whether he can be put to use in the analysis of sexism and oppression or whether he stands to be accused of misogyny and sexism. The editor of the volume seeks to show that beyond the easy critiques that can be made to Sartre, his thought actually can be used in a feminist context as he was one of the first to make gender a philosophical issue.

François Noudelmann et Gilles Philippe (dir.) (2004) *Dictionnaire Sartre*. Paris: Honoré-Champion

This is an invaluable tool for beginners as well as scholars of Sartre. The dictionary contains encyclopedia-like entries on themes, concepts, writings, and persons that are relevant to the study of Sartre. These entries are more than strict dictionary definitions. Rather, they provide a definition as well as an in-depth analysis of the item discussed. These entries have been written by an impressive list of Sartre scholars who have contributed their various expertise in all things Sartrean. A must for Sartre research.

Benedict O'Donohoe (2005) *Sartre's Theatre: Acts for Life*. Bern: Peter Lang

This book is the most exhaustive study of Sartre's theater to appear in English. It offers an analysis of each play written by Sartre while providing details regarding the context of each play and of its reception. O'Donohoe offers his own understanding of the theatrical endeavor in Sartre and its relation to the philosophical one in his introduction. A must for anyone interested in Sartre as a playwright but also for those, like me, who like to use the plays to illustrate the philosophical concepts.

Alistair Rolls and Elizabeth Rechniewski (eds.) (2005) *Sartre's* Nausea. *Text, Context, Intertext*. Amsterdam: Rodopi

This collection of essays ensues from a conference that examined Sartre's novel *Nausea* from various and new perspectives. The articles therein provide scholarly analyses of themes to be found in the novel such as art and illumination, the role of others, the subject as symptom, meaningful existence, and contingency.

Peter Royle (1982) *The Sartre–Camus Controversy. A Literary and Philosophical Critique*. Ottawa: University of Ottawa Press

In this essay, Royle explores the differences between Camus and Sartre as they come to be expressed in literary works such as *Nausea*, *The Wall*, *The Outsider*, and *The Plague*. Royle begins his analysis with Camus' *The Rebel*, the publication of which led to the break between Sartre and Camus. However, the essay demonstrates that philosophical differences were already in place.

Ronald E. Santoni (2003) *Sartre on Violence. Curiously Ambivalent*. University Park (PA): Penn State University Press

In this book, Santoni offers an in-depth analysis of the concept of violence as we find it in the various writings of Sartre. The book contains two parts, the first being dedicated to Sartre's views on violence as they are expressed first in *Being and Nothingness* but also in later works such as the *Critique of Dialectical Reason*. The second part examines the Camus–Sartre confrontation on the necessity of violence and its limits. The study shows that the problem of violence was great for Sartre and one that he could not leave unaddressed.

Sartre Studies International. An Interdisciplinary Journal of Existentialism and Contemporary Culture

Since 1995, the North American Sartre Society and the United Kingdom Society for Sartrean Studies have published two issues per year. This peer-reviewed journal publishes scholarly articles on any and every aspect of Sartre's work. The journal also offers book reviews and a bulletin board that keeps track of all activities, conferences, exhibits, publications, that pertain to Sartre.

Paul Arthur Schilpp (ed.) (1981) *The Philosophy of Jean-Paul Sartre*. LaSalle (Illinois): Open Court, The Library of Living Philosophers, Vol. XVI

This is another important collection of essays that contains scholarly articles by noted Sartre scholars as well as by philosopher Paul Ricoeur. It differs from others in that it contains a lengthy interview with Sartre at the beginning of the book that was conducted by Rybalka, Pucciani, and Gruenheck in May 1975. A bibliography prepared by Michel Rybalka is also included in the book.

Hugh J. Silverman and Frederick A. Elliston (eds.) (1980) *Jean-Paul Sartre. Contemporary Approaches to his Philosophy*. Pittsburgh: Duquesne University Press

This collection of essays presents scholarly analyses of important themes and problems in Sartre's philosophy. The first section tackles existential-phenomenological themes like the phenomenological reduction, bad faith, the body, and freedom. The second section addresses philosophical problems such as the self, the imaginary, meaning in art, and history, while the third part compares Sartre with other philosophers like Husserl, Heidegger, Marx, and Merleau-Ponty. The book thus covers many bases and key problems in Sartrean scholarship.

Philip Thody and Howard Read (1998) *Introducing Sartre*. Cambridge: Icon Books

Another introductory book that adopts a different approach. Each theme is dealt with in two pages with a little text and cartoonish illustrations to accompany and explain the theme under discussion. It covers the basics of Sartre's philosophy as well as important publications of his.

Craig Vasey (ed.) (2009) *The Last Chance: Roads of Freedom Volume IV*. Edited and translated by Craig Vasey. London: Continuum Press

Sartre's trilogy, *The Roads to Freedom*, is not a trilogy but a quadrilogy! Sartre had begun drafting a fourth volume in which the characters of Brunet and Mathieu meet again in a prisoner of war camp. While such drafts were available in the Pléiade edition of Sartre's *Oeuvres Romanesques*, this is the first time the English reader has access to the texts. They are accompanied by commentaries by the editor as well as documents pertaining to the fourth volume.

WORKS CITED

Anderson, Thomas C. *The Foundation and Structure of Sartrean Ethics*. Lawrence: The Regents Press of Kansas, 1979.

—— *Sartre's Two Ethics: From Authenticity to Integral Humanity*. Chicago and LaSalle: Open Court, 1993.

Barnes, Hazel. "Translator's Introduction" in Sartre, Jean-Paul. *Being and Nothingness*. New York: Washington Square Press, 1992, pp. ix–lii.

De Beauvoir, Simone. *The Ethics of Ambiguity*. Trans. Bernard Frechtman, New York: Citadel Press, 1976.

—— *Force of Circumstance*. Trans. Richard Howard, London: Readers Union, 1966.

—— *Philosophical Writings*. Edited by Margaret A. Simons, Urbana and Chicago: University of Illinois Press, 2004.

—— *The Prime of Life*. Trans. Peter Green, Harmondsworth: Penguin Books, 1962.

—— *The Second Sex*. Trans. H. M. Parshley. New York: Vintage, 1989.

Boulé, Jean-Pierre. *Sartre, Self-Formation and Masculinities*. New York and Oxford: Berghahn Books, 2005.

—— "Sartrean Structuralism?" in Howells, Christina (ed.). *The Cambridge Companion to Sartre*. Cambridge: Cambridge University Press, 1992, pp. 293–317.

Catalano, Joseph S. *A Commentary on Jean-Paul Sartre's* Critique of Dialectical Reason, *volume 1, Theory of Practical Ensembles*. Chicago and London: The University of Chicago Press, 1986.

Caws, Peter. *Sartre*. London: Routledge, 1979.

Cohen-Solal, Annie. *Jean-Paul Sartre: A Life*. New York: New Press, 2005.

Daigle, Christine and Jacob Golomb (eds.). *Beauvoir and Sartre: The Riddle of Influence*. Bloomington: Indiana University Press, 2009.

Drake, David. *Sartre*. London: Haus Publishing, 2005.

Flynn, Thomas R. "L'Imagination au pouvoir: The Evolution of Sartre's Political and Social Thought," *Political Theory*, vol. 7, May 1979, pp. 157–80.

Foucault, Michel. *Dits et écrits*, volume 1, Paris: Gallimard, 2001.

Gerassi, John. *Jean-Paul Sartre: Hated Conscience of His Century*. Chicago: University of Chicago Press, 1989.

Grene, Marjorie. "Authenticity: an Existential Virtue," *Ethics*, 62, 4, 1951/52, pp. 266–74.

Howells, Christina. "Conclusion: Sartre and the Deconstruction of the Subject" in Howells, Christina (ed.). *The Cambridge Companion to Sartre*. Cambridge: Cambridge University Press, 1992, pp. 318–52.

Kruks, Sonia. "Simone de Beauvoir: Teaching Sartre About Freedom" in Ron Aronson and Adrian van den Hoven (eds.), *Sartre Alive*, Detroit: Wayne State University Press, 1991.

Lévy, Bernard-Henri. *Sartre: The Philosopher of the Twentieth Century*. Cambridge: Polity Press, 2003.

McBride, William. "The Sartre Centenary: Why Sartre Now?" in L. Embree and T. Nenon (eds.) *Phenomenology 2005, Vol. IV, Selected Essays from North America*. Bucharest: Zeta Books, 2007.

Martin, Thomas. *Oppression and the Human Condition. An Introduction to Sartrean Existentialism*. Lanham: Rowman & Littlefield, 2002.

Merleau-Ponty, Maurice. *Phenomenology of Perception*. Trans. Colin Smith. London: Routledge, 1962.

Murphy, Julien S. "Introduction" in Murphy, Julien S. (ed.). *Feminist Interpretations of Jean-Paul Sartre*. University Park (PA); Pennsylvania State University Press, 1999, pp. 1–21

Noudelmann, François et Gilles Philippe (dir.). *Dictionnaire Sartre*. Paris: Honoré-Champion, 2004.

Olafson, Frederick A. "Jean-Paul Sartre" in Edwards, Paul (ed.). *The Encyclopedia of Philosophy*. Vol. 7. New York: The MacMillan Co. & The Free Press, 1967, pp. 287–93.

Rybalka, Michel, Oreste Pucciani, and Susan Gruenheck, "An Interview with Jean-Paul Sartre (May 12 and May 19, 1975), P.A. Schilpp (ed.) *The Philosophy of Jean-Paul Sartre*. LaSalle (Illinois): Open Court, 1981.

Santoni, Ronald E. *Sartre on Violence: Curiously Ambivalent*. University Park (Pennsylvania): Penn State University Press, 2003.

Sartre, Jean-Paul. "Childhood of a Leader," *The Wall (Intimacy) and Other Stories*. Trans. Lloyd Alexander. New York: New Directions, 1975.

—— *Literary and Philosophical Essays*. Trans. Annette Michelson, New York: Collier Books, 1967.

—— "Le Réformisme et les fétiches," *Situations VII*, Paris: Gallimard, [1956] 1965.

—— "La République du silence" (9 septembre 1944), *Situations III*, Paris: Gallimard, 1949.

—— *Théâtre complet*, Paris, Gallimard, La Pléiade, 2005.

—— *La Transcendance de l'Ego et autres textes phénoménologiques*. Textes introduits et annotés par Vincent de Coorebyter. Paris: Vrin, 2003.

Sartre, Jean-Paul et Michel Sicard. "Entretien. L'écriture et la publication." *Obliques*. Numéro special 18–19, 1979, pp. 9–29.

Simont, Juliette. "Sartrean Ethics" in Howells, Christina (ed.). *The Cambridge Companion to Sartre*. Cambridge: Cambridge University Press, 1992, pp. 178–210.

"Sartre, Jean-Paul" (Sartre's intervention in the debate) *Que peut la littérature?* présentation par Yves Buin, Paris: Union Générale d'éditions, coll. L'Inédit 10/18, 1965, pp. 107–27.

Young, Robert C. "Preface to *The Wretched of the Earth*" in Sartre, *Colonialism and neocolonialism*. New York: Routledge, 2006, pp. 153–174.

INDEX